Matching and Dispatching

Matching and Dispatching

*Wedding and Funeral Stories of a
Battle-Toughened Pastor*

JAMES O. CHATHAM

Foreword by
JOHN KUYKENDALL

[signature: James O. Chatham]

WIPF & STOCK · Eugene, Oregon

MATCHING AND DISPATCHING
Wedding and Funeral Stories of a Battle-Toughened Pastor

Wipf & Stock
An Imprint of Wipf and Stock Publishers
199 W. 8th Ave., Suite 3
Eugene, OR 97401

www.wipfandstock.com

ISBN 13: 978-1-61097-871-2

Manufactured in the U.S.A.

An earlier version of Chapter 10, "A Garland Instead of Ashes," was previously published in *Sundays Down South*, University Press of Mississippi. Used here by permission.

To Nancy,
the treasure of my life

Contents

Contents

Foreword

"THE MAIN territory of the pastor is human life, the most valuable thing on the planet."[1]

The person who wrote the words quoted above has a grasp of their significance as well as anyone I know. In his decades as a parish minister, James O. Chatham embodied the sort of caring presence that convinced those around him that he both understood and loved that "main territory" with all his being. As a pastor, he demonstrated a rare capacity for *really* knowing the people around him in his church, and he was both willing and able to extend the bounds of that parish far beyond the membership roll of his congregation. As will be evident from several of the episodes in this book, Jim served as a sort of "minister without portfolio" to the larger community which surrounded the parishes he served in Mississippi, North Carolina, Ohio and Kentucky.

Jim Chatham went off to college in his native North Carolina with every intention to become an electrical engineer. Even as he pursued graduate studies in his chosen field, many around him recognized that he had all the gifts and graces which combined with his strong faith to make him a natural for the ministry. In the providence of God, he made the decision to enter the ministry. This tall—*very* tall—and gentle man conveys by his posture and countenance that he both hears and understands the stories of joy and sorrow which have been shared with him by "all sorts and conditions" of people whose lives intersect with his. If there be

1. Chatham, James O. *Is It I, Lord? Discerning God's Call To Be a Pastor.* (Louisville: Westminster John Knox, 2002), 12.

such a thing as "a pastoral heart"—and I am convinced that there is—Jim has personified it in his life and ministry.

The pastoral heart surely has many characteristics and dimensions, and salient among those several gifts is a balance between empathy and compassion on the one hand and a keen sense of humor on the other. Jim recognizes that it is often the case that both of these gifts come into play in the pastor's life in times of special significance, such as weddings and funerals: "matching" and "dispatching" as the old joke goes. Laughter and tears are closer to the surface at such times than they are in the regular rounds of life, and the inherently memorable nature of those occasions will often be enriched by recollections of occurrences which may not—or may!— have been a part of the plan for the ceremony.

Many of Jim Chatham's stories have been shaped substantially by the particular setting in which they occurred. In most cases, that setting is the American South, and regardless of what the future may hold, for our generation it is a fact that Southern religion has been and is a distinctive variation on the national theme. Thus there is a certain uniqueness to the expectations of Southerners insofar as religious ceremonies are concerned. Many of those peculiar expectations are reflected in the stories you are about to read. This is not to say that only Southerners will understand or enjoy what's going on, but, as Flannery O'Connor once said about her own storytelling, it may occasionally feel as though God is speaking with a southern accent.

More than once in his years of ministry, Jim Chatham was probably tempted to say, "Now I've seen it all!" But he surely knew better, and likely he also probably had a premonition that such an assertion would have only been tempting fate (or providence) to prove him wrong. The stories he tells in *Matching and Dispatching* seem to insist that there is always another surprise waiting just around the corner. All these tales are true; all derive from the pastoral experience of one person; and, allowing for the bit of narrative latitude which any good story-teller richly deserves, the stories are the unvarnished truth. Sometimes the next episode will have a poignancy which bespeaks the marvelous complexity and contingency of the human condition. Other times there can be no alternative for the reader except to laugh out loud at "what fools these mortals be!" Thus the rich fare which awaits you in the following pages will frequently make you laugh, and occasionally it might also bring you the point of tears. In either case, it will surely give you the privilege of observing both the compassion and the creativity of a very special person who has been a true pastor to the people he has *matched and dispatched.*

John Kuykendall,
Davidson, North Carolina

Acknowledgments

I wish to thank Nancy Chatham, my wife, whose perspective on these tales was second-to-none since she was intimately a part of it all. She alone knew what fundamental questions to ask, the broad changes to suggest, how to meet difficult challenges, what wisdom to invoke, and what stories the book did and did not need to include. She put up with the endless hours I spent buried in "the nest." She corrected scores of my mistakes. And, most of all, she remained enthusiastic about the manuscript, providing a motivation matched by no other.

I acknowledge the talented and tireless efforts of Elizabeth Byerly who copy-edited the manuscript in nearly microscopic detail, twice. Her keen knowledge and experience made what you will read seem far more natural and good. I stand in awe of the high quality of Elizabeth's work.

I thank Diana Chatham Calaway, "big sister," who, as an English professor, scanned the work with keen eyes and a discerning heart, helping to form its final shape.

And I express my appreciation to the members of Highland Presbyterian Church, Louisville, Kentucky, who, over our twenty-five year relationship, provided the main substance and character for this book. Matchings and dispatchings occur in many varieties, and we went through it all together.

Introduction

CAVE HILL Cemetery is a stately, dignified, 150-year-old burial ground in Louisville, Kentucky. Situated in The Highlands just east of downtown, it provides the final resting place for senators and congressmen, mayors, governors, several hundred Civil War soldiers, Meriwether Clark (of Lewis and Clark fame), Colonel Harlan Sanders, and a variety of others.

My friend Millie Hunter was attending a funeral at Cave Hill. The burial site was on a hillside. The party of mourners parked on the road above and made its way down. En route, Millie stepped in a hole hidden by grass and leaves. She tumbled forward, landing on her side and injuring her hip. The Emergency Medical Service was summoned. Within minutes, the rescue van came through the cemetery gate and arrived at the site.

The medical crew went to work quickly and efficiently, assessing Millie's condition and easing her onto a gurney. As they moved her up the hill toward the van, one seasoned medic looked at her and quipped, "Lady, I've carried a lot of people into this place, but you're the first one I've ever carried out." According to Millie, that nearly made the accident worthwhile.

Old Southern wisdom states that the preacher is needed mostly for three occasions: baptisms, weddings, and funerals. Some wag labeled this, "for hatching, matching, and dispatching." The baptisms are great: cute babies and proud, adoring families. But it's the matchings and dispatchings that produce the stories. Weddings and funerals are both highly ritualized proceedings in which all major events were scripted long ago. Cultural

1

expectations make fairly certain what will happen. Now and again, however, the unexpected intrudes, sometimes boldly. The intrusions have created this book.

I have written from the pastor's vantage point. Weddings and funerals look one way to the families, an entirely different way to the pastor in charge. For families, a wedding is a joyous celebration for launching a promising couple into marital happiness, a blow-the-budget, once-in-a-lifetime event designed to be as perfect as the planners can make it. The ideal is to create a dream day for the bride and groom, a moment they will never forget. Funerals are heavy experiences that promise sadness and ask endurance. The purpose is to get through and survive, hopefully feeling more faithful and trusting, but definitely with *loss* as the dominant theme.

The pastor has an entirely different angle. While empathizing deeply with those involved, the pastor must be the total-event architect. He/she must take a sometimes strange assortment of human wishes, relationships, and emotions, plus a bizarre gathering of theological beliefs and cultural expectations, and weave from them a whole experience which is good. Usually, that works out very well. Not always.

I had a groom who wanted to end his very formal church wedding by issuing a resounding whistle, at which his two large hound dogs would come galloping down the aisle to join him and his wife, then to accompany them back up the aisle in their departure. Fortunately, the best man was the son of the chairman of the church's property committee, which had recently installed new sanctuary carpet, and the question was decisively resolved without my having to say a word. I wondered what the groom had in mind for their wedding night.

A bride brought to her Friday afternoon wedding her Hitachi boom box, wanting me to set it on a ledge behind me and punch it as the service began, providing sentimental background music by artists she liked. Her favorite was John Denver. There was no way I could compete with "Country Roads, Take Me Home," "Sunshine on My Shoulders," and "Thank God I'm a Country Boy."

At one wedding, the groom sat with his guitar on a stool at the front of the sanctuary serenading his wife-to-be with love songs as she gracefully moved down the aisle (she was a dancer/actress), all of which was quite beautiful and touching. Their three-year-old son sat cross-legged on the front pew, amazed that he had never seen Mommy and Daddy act this way before.

A young bride asked her college roommate, a violin player, to perform a solo in her December wedding, only to have the hundred-year-old church's steam radiators turn on and start banging fifteen feet away. It totally shattered the violinist's nerves and wrecked her performance. We had to stop the wedding to let the bride comfort her sobbing friend.

A bride in her forties, a mother of four getting married for the third time, wanted to wear a white bridal dress with veil and train, and to come down the aisle on her father's arm, after which he would give her away. She explained that this was compensation for her having eloped on her first two marriages and her belief that following the standard ritual might be more pleasing to God and make things work out better the third time.

As I spoke the words, "I now pronounce you husband and wife," one beautiful bride squeezed the hand of her handsome, powerfully built, Naval Academy graduate husband so hard that she broke his middle finger, bending it sideways across his newly placed wedding ring. It hurts to think of spending your first married evening in the emergency room because of your bride's enthusiasm.

I gently placed my hand on a groom's shoulder to shift his position during the wedding rehearsal. This tightly strung emergency room doctor pulled away, looked up at me and scowled, "I'll thank you to keep your hands off me!" I thought to myself, "Are you sure you want to marry him?" looking at the young nurse from my congregation who was about to become his wife. I suspected that further chapters in this relationship were yet to come.

One couple seemed intent on including in their wedding every cockeyed idea their minds had ever thought of. They wanted the guests treated to hors d'oeuvres and wine in the back of the sanctuary. They wanted the bridesmaids and bride to make a royal entry beneath a canopy from a limousine well stocked with what they called "anxiety fortification." They wanted their ushers dressed in red, Scotch plaid jackets with white shirts and black bow ties. They wanted their wedding to include testimonies from friends on what a perfect, made-in-heaven match this marriage was, even though both of them had been sleeping around for years, and would continue. They wanted a helicopter to land in the church parking lot to ferry them to their downtown reception. I had the feeling we were swashing a veneer of cheap plaster over the fundamental weaknesses in their relationship, which neither of them wanted to face. (The only reason I consented to conduct this wedding was that her mother was our neighbor.) Throughout the proceeding, I was just "the religion guy," a necessity required by tradition and law. Rarely have I felt so disregarded. They had said they were headed for a career in hotel management, the up-scale hospitality industry. It was a hotel I would not want to stay in.

In the "dispatching" realm, I was notified one day that a ninety-year-old member of my congregation had died at her home. She had been a high school math teacher, never married. She had lived alone in a small, two-story frame house near the school where she had taught. When I arrived at her house, I was greeted by a funeral home director who invited me inside. We sat in the living room talking about arrangements. After a bit, there was the noise of footsteps on the narrow winding staircase behind us. I turned to see a man making his way down the staircase, a funeral home employee. It took me a moment for me to realize that he was carrying the dead woman crumpled across his arms. He reached the bottom of the stairs and set her in a seated position on the sofa beside me. Then, seeing me for the first time, he winced, "Oh, I'm sorry. I didn't know anyone else was down here. That staircase was too narrow to bring her down on a gurney." In the next few minutes, we completed our negotiations, the only funeral I have ever planned seated next to the corpse. I kept expecting her to speak up and say what she wanted.

Through forty years of matching and dispatching, the pastor sees beauty, devotion, joy, pain, struggle, grief, humor, banality, incredibly poor taste, and disgusting ugliness, all of which occur in this book.

∾

My career as a pastor began in Jefferson County, Mississippi, where I led two small churches, the Fayette and Union Church Presbyterian churches. Fayette was a mini-plantation community deeply imbedded in the traditions of the Old South. Even though the population was eighty percent African-American, one hundred percent of the town's leadership was white, and everything except the downtown sidewalks was segregated. After civil rights figure Charles Evers took over the town in the late 1960s, it completely changed character, most of the former leaders selling their property and departing for other places.

Union Church was a tiny village surrounded by family farms. The hardworking people who populated that countryside were grounded in the soil, having only moderate concern over the issues raging in the outer world. They quietly scorned "all those high-society, plantation people in Fayette," thinking of them as rich and pampered. Being the grandson of a North Carolina tobacco farmer, I knew innately the folkways of Union Church and felt much at home.

Moving to Winston-Salem, North Carolina, I spent a seven-year pastorate in a struggling low-income ghetto, the former Reynolds Tobacco Company labor village. Some of the most intelligent and resourceful human beings I have ever known lived in that neighborhood, people who had honed the skills of surviving in poverty. The main thing I learned was to appreciate lives of simple devotion, folks who knew, loved, and cared for one another while possessing almost nothing.

For three years I was in Columbus, Ohio, working in a partially white-collar, partially blue-collar congregation within walking distance of the Ohio State University campus. The region had produced governors, senators, Presidents, medical experts, golf champions, football stars, CEOs, top musicians, and an astronaut. Super-success was the purpose of life. The community possessed only questionable tolerance toward those who weren't going to achieve it. I spent three years shoring up the lives of normal, average teenage kids who weren't. They were aware at every turn that their future was filled with question marks.

In Louisville, Kentucky, I led a talented, upper-middle class, 1200-member church for twenty-five years. Through every imaginable human saga, the church transitioned from a country club congregation of cultural elites into a much younger, more vigorous, less wealthy assemblage of professional moderates and progressives.

In this book I have changed many names, seeking privacy for people to whom I think it will matter. In a couple of cases I have refashioned whole stories to hide identities but still make the narrative point. With well-known persons I have used real names.

Please be aware that I am telling the stories *as I remember them*, what the literary field calls "narrative truth." I have not researched the stories factually. In many cases that would be impossible, in others quite useless.

Manuscript readers have told me that it is not easy to bounce back and forth between wedding and funeral emotions. I therefore have gathered the "matching" stories into the first part of the book and the "dispatching" stories into the second. If you want variety, feel free to do your own bouncing. All it takes is two bookmarks.

A few observations on weddings. For some enigmatic reason, many of the most forward-thinking, modern-age young couples in America want to go totally retro in planning their own weddings. They approach every other area of life with contemporary ideas, but they anchor this ceremony firmly in tradition. They want to take several of their young men friends, dress them in starched, stiff penguin suits, train them in nineteenth century gallantry, and have them show attending ladies to their seats with husbands trailing dutifully and uselessly behind. They want to dress several young women in expensive, unique-design, formal outfits they will never wear again, bring them one-by-one down the aisle look-ing extremely self-conscious and out-of-place, and stand them at the front serving approximately the same function as the banks of flowers that form the backdrop. They want to dress the bride in a glowing white outfit with veil and train, symbolizing the un-tarnished purity of her innocent youthfulness. They want to have the bride's father "give her away," implying that she has previously been his property which he is now turning over to another domi-nant male. They want to "pledge their troth" to each other, even though neither one has the slightest idea what that means. She may be a tough-minded, hard-driving business woman who brooks no slack in attaining the company goals, and he may be an amiable critter with little more initiative than to find his way out of bed in the morning, and they may have been living together for three years. But, at wedding time, the odds are very high that they will submerge all current realities in tradition and do it the way they imagine grandmother did it. I have stopped asking why.

Funerals are essentially command performances. Nearly everyone in the family comes no matter what, all the relatives who love one another plus the others who don't. This can make for intense dynamics. The most emotionally complicated funeral I ever led involved two daughters of their deceased mother. Both daughters had, several years before, divorced their husbands quite acrimoniously and then remarried. The bite was that each had remarried the other's former spouse, with whom she had been having an affair before her divorce. There were cold, steely stares all across the funeral parlor. I kept waiting for the volcano to erupt, issuing a sigh of relief when it didn't! Mama still commanded the power to keep her girls separated, even after she was dead.

A funeral can provide unique and extremely valuable opportunity. There was a family of two sisters and a brother whose mother had died. The day before the funeral, I sat the three of them down in a living room to talk about Mom. "Tell me your most vivid memories." There ensued a two-hour family portrait of touching beauty: laughing, crying, pain, pleasure, joy, fulfillment, frustration, and peace. Several days later, one of the daughters called me. "Jim, you didn't know it, but you saw a miracle the other afternoon. Brother Tom hasn't spoken a dozen words to either of us sisters in twenty years. He got out of sorts back when we were young and has cut himself off ever since. Tuesday was the breakthrough. He's been a different person ever since." Great family loss can also lead to great family gain.

Funerals have a special quality no pastor should forget. Regardless of the deceased's life, at the funeral the pastor had best speak only one thing: what we have to be thankful for from this person's time on earth. The deceased may have been chronically unfaithful to four successive spouses, may have been an alcoholic who left relational garbage littered down a lifelong trail, may have been a brazen crook who embezzled thousands of dollars from struggling retirees, or may have been so annoyingly garrulous that everyone constantly wanted to escape. There is no need in mentioning any of this at the funeral! *All human beings have exhibited good somewhere in their lives; find it and give thanks for it*: the preacher's best advice! Only the fool will think that honesty is the best policy.

PART ONE
Matching

1

Candid Granny

THE EXTENDED family of Hazelwoods, three generations, shared one prominent characteristic: they were all garrulous. *They loved to talk!* A quiet moment was anathema. And, further, their minds were an open page. The slightest glimmer that walked through someone's head you were going to hear. Hazelwood genes contained no propriety filter, no concern for effect, just a super-highway from brain to tongue. Flattering or offensive, bitter or sweet, refined or crude, when a Hazelwood spoke, you knew you were getting the real thing. In the South, where a major art-form is to be thinking one thing but to say exactly the opposite, it could be refreshing.

Young Marvin Hazelwood showed up with good news! "I'm getting married! To Ellen Rose Burk. You've met Ellen Rose a couple of times after church. She's a short brunette who works in the public information booth at the airport. She's really nice, relates to people well, cheerful and friendly. It comes naturally to her. We've been going together for a year now and have decided to make it permanent. She's from a big family and so am I. Five brothers and sisters to match my four. Aunts and uncles everywhere. It will be a marriage of two populations, villages merging. We'll have the wedding at the church and the reception at Audubon Park Country Club. We wondered about the low-flying airplanes since the country club is just off the end of an airport runway, but we went out there and checked at the same time of day, and we don't think it will be a problem. The country club is really beautiful, and extra flowers and plants make it look like a southern garden. Ellen Rose's older sister is a decorator, and she will be in charge of decorations. I have one cousin in California who won't be able to come, but it looks like everyone else can make it. Ellen Rose has in mind a big wedding, and I go along with that. We both love being surrounded by people, especially family." Marvin stopped only when the well ran completely dry.

"That's wonderful, Marvin," I said, "I wish both of you a very happy life together."

"We want you to perform our marriage," he said.

"I will be honored and delighted," I replied.

Marvin had spent time in seminary, and he was a fairly sentimental guy. The two of them wanted their wedding to include nearly everything they had ever experienced in a worship service that had been meaningful to them: Bible readings, hymns, quotations from favorite authors, a flute solo, a full length sermon, the lighting of a unity candle, and a congregational affirmation of faith. The list was long.

I offered the gentle warning that we might be looking at a lot of time. They replied, "This only happens once. We'll use as much time as it needs." So be it.

On the appointed Saturday afternoon, a huge aggregation of family and friends gathered. The seating of family took nearly fifteen minutes. The entry of the groomsmen was about the only quick-and-simple thing that happened. The entry of the bridesmaids followed, all eight processing very slowly. In the unrolling of a white carpet, the roller stuck, and two friends had to struggle to fix it. The ring bearer and the flower girl were cute, as they always are.

Wedding march. Bride escorted by father. Call to worship. Prayer. Hymn. Reading. I glanced around to see if I could find a watch visible on someone's arm. I did. Thirty-nine minutes had gone by, and we had a distance to go. Bible reading. Hymn. Sermon. Flute.

It was at this time that I became aware that someone was moving out in the sanctuary, at one o'clock in my vision. I looked up and found the movement: an older woman dressed in elegant wedding attire, a bluish-gray dress, white gloves, and a hat. Marvin's grandmother appeared stately and dignified on the third row. She was rising slowly from her seat. She consumed a considerable expanse and was impossible not to see.

About half way up, she paused, looked left, looked right, scanned to see the attitudes on faces around her, and then spoke with determined force, "When the hell is this goddamned wedding going to be over with?"

No one laughed. A number of us gagged trying not to. It was the question in many minds! "Thanks, grandma! You said it exactly right!" Vintage, Hazelwood.

2

Holy Crow! What Have I Done?

Annabelle Hargis belonged to my church, a woman probably fifty-four. She had been married twice previously and had adult children. Annabelle hired herself out to care for elderly people in their homes. She was a natural: a devoted heart, empathetic, with a pleasant disposition, plus strong and vigorous.

Edgar Rowan appeared to be an uncomplicated man, a nice guy who moved through life doing his best. About five years older than Annabelle, he was employed in a mattress factory, clipping into place little springs, joints, and curlicues that all added up to providing a comfortable night's sleep. Edgar was in no way verbose, tending to watch and listen far more than he talked. I got the impression that Annabelle might be doing pretty well her third time around.

Only a few family members came to the wedding. We stood in the front of the church sanctuary on a Friday afternoon clustered together. Edgar said his vows and Annabelle hers. I declared that they were husband and wife, executing the marriage license. All went well, and this mid-life couple launched into their new relationship.

Monday morning, my phone was ringing as I walked into my office. The female voice on the other end said, "Hello. Are you the church reverend?"

"Yes ma'am, I am," I replied.

"According to the newspaper Annabelle Hargis and Edgar Rowan were married in your church last Friday. Did you perform the marriage?"

"Yes, ma'am, I did," I said.

"Well, did you know that Edgar Rowan is still married to me? My name is Frances Rowan, and we were never divorced."

"No ma'am, I most certainly did not know that, Mrs. Rowan, but it sounds like somebody has a problem."

"He certainly does have a problem," she said. "Last I heard, it's illegal to be married to two people at the same time."

"I'd say it is, Mrs. Rowan. Somebody has blundered."

"Reverend, I'll call you back when we need to talk further," she said. "I've got some checking around to do. Y'all can't just go do this on a whim. He's still my husband." I wondered where she intended to go with it.

I told my law school professor friend, Ron Eades, about this situation, and he wrote it up for presentation to his torts class as a case study. Under Kentucky law, does the preacher bear liability for performing the marriage of an already married person? A few weeks earlier, Ron had sent me a one-page flier he had received from his alma mater, the Harvard Law School, announcing a seminar on "ecclesiastical torts," inviting alums to "come and learn all about this exciting new field." Across the bottom of the flier, Ron had penned a message, "You'll be fine if you'll do what Jesus told you to do: give it all away." I have to admit a measure of anxiety. Weeks later, toward the end of their semester, Ron's class concluded that as long as the pastor was presented with a duly drawn marriage license executed by the State, he/she bears no responsibility for determining the marital status of the two parties. I was relieved.

Mrs. Rowan never called back.

3

With Sammy Sosa Attending

SAMMY SOSA: outfielder, Texas Rangers, then the Chicago White Sox, then the Chicago Cubs, then the Baltimore Orioles; 588 career home runs, sixty-four in one season with the Cubs eclipsing the all-time major league record set more than seventy years earlier by Babe Ruth. George W. Bush, former owner of the Texas Rangers and President of the United States, when asked by a news reporter to name a mistake he had made somewhere in his life, answered, "Trading Sammy Sosa." How many of us can say that Sammy Sosa attended our wedding?

There was indecision: where do we hold the ceremony? In church, the traditional place? On a hilltop with the sun going down? Maybe here? Maybe there? No verdict. The date had been set: 9/9/99 (easy to remember), but not the place. Son Andy would call often from Dallas on Sunday nights.

"You and Misti reach any answer yet?" we would ask.

"Naw, we're still working on it."

"Any closer?"

"Don't know."

It was May. Time was running short. That same Sunday evening telephone conversation replayed week after week. Finally, one night, on a whim, I, his father, said to Andy at the end of the exchange, "Why don't you transcend the whole dilemma and get married in the right field bleacher at Wrigley Field during a Cub game?" What a wacko comment! I couldn't believe I had said it. But what I really couldn't believe was what happened next. Dead silence. Not a sound. "Oh no! He's taking me seriously! Can't be! Not really!"

"*Dad, that is a great idea!*"

"Andy, I wasn't . . . !"

"Dad, that is fantastic! Why didn't we think of that before? That will solve everything!"

"Andy!"

Always our center-of-the-action child. On the way to school, other little kids would find dimes and quarters at the bus stop; Andy would find twenty dollar bills. On the high school baseball team, he started in left field, got the coach to move him to third base because there wasn't enough happening in left field, and then switched to catcher because the catcher is in the middle of every play. Never at a loss for words, destined to be a courtroom lawyer, quick on his feet, kills Jeopardy, ideas no one else would ever think of, restless in the pauses, tantalized by the bizarre. "Andy, not really?"

"*Dad, that is a great idea!*"

Too late. No stuffing the toothpaste back in the tube. Why had I said it? Just joking! That's what you think. Boom! Here we go.

Andy and Misti had met in law school at Oklahoma City University. She was from the tiny town of Hollis in the southwest corner of Oklahoma, daughter of a public school teacher mother and a very enterprising farmer father. They had known each other through graduation, started going together, and now wanted to get married.

By some miraculous process to which I was not privy, Andy gained the consent, if not the enthusiastic endorsement, of all parties involved. Even Misti seemed genuinely happy. (Misti's devotions are to the Dallas Cowboys, not the Chicago Cubs.) The wedding would be in the right field bleachers of Wrigley Field,

17

Chicago, Illinois, September 9, 1999. Chicago Cubs versus the Cincinnati Reds. It was a game the Cubs might have some chance of winning, though probably not.

Andy had become an avid Cub fan at age six. We had lived in Columbus, Ohio, beside a family from Chicago with three boys and three girls. The boys had eaten and breathed Cub baseball, certain that Bill Matlock, the power-hitting third baseman, was the greatest sports hero God had ever anointed. Andy had soaked it all in, believing every word the older boys said. By the time we had moved from Columbus, he was a 100 percent addicted, unwavering Cub devotee.

Cub fans have a special quality no outsider will ever understand. The Cubs, no matter how much talent they possess or how much promise they offer, maintain an uncanny capacity to lose. Whether it's by going dead and dropping a six game lead in the final twelve days of the season, or by having their own fan lean out of the stands to deflect a fly ball and deprive them of victory in the National League playoff. No matter how, the Cubs always lose. The miracle is that through the anguish, the disillusionment, the frustration, the howls, the complaints, the agony, and the soul wringings, Cub fans continue to adore their team! They love their heroes: Greg Maddux, Ryan Sandburg, Andre Dawson, Ferguson Jenkins, to name but a few. They love old, rickety Wrigley Field (yes, the chewing gum magnate). They love being located in a one-hundred-year-old, blue-collar, northside Chicago neighborhood that fills the stadium every game with laborers who work hard, sweat profusely, drink heartily, and believe that America's national game belongs to the masses, not to a glassed-in elite in air-conditioned corporate sky boxes. They love the tradition in which radio announcer Harry Caray used to take the public address microphone during the seventh inning stretch and declare, "Okay, Cub fans, let's hear it! Ah-one, ah-two, ah-three: Take me out to the ballgame," thus leading the assembled throng in a badly out-of-tune version of the Cub Nation anthem, a tradition that continues under other luminaries now that Harry Caray is dead. The team has a long history of starting with a burst and ending with a whimper, but this in no measure dampens Cub fan ardor. To be ever faithful champions of what everyone knows is a lost cause, that is the Cub ethos.

By our next phone conversation a week later, Andy had bought fifty bleacher tickets for 9/9/99. When he had commented to the ticket sales person, "My fiancee and I plan to get married there that afternoon," the reply had been, "You can't do that!" Andy had asked, "Why not?" To which the voice had replied, "Well, for one thing, you'll never find a priest willing to lead it." Andy had responded, "Want to bet?"

Families and friends began scrambling for Southwest Airlines cheap seats into Chicago, all of us radiantly looking forward to the wedding. People from everywhere wanted to come, acquaintances close and distant, unlikely family members, folks who simply thought it was a great idea and didn't want to miss it.

Nancy and I found a little 1920s vintage ex-gangster hotel three blocks south of Wrigley Field on Belmont Avenue and essentially booked the entire place. A block away was a restaurant adequate for a rehearsal dinner the night before where we would have a more serious ceremonial on the meaning of marriage.

The wedding itself exceeded all our hopes and wishes! Fifty-two guests came from Oklahoma, Kentucky, Alabama, Missouri, Maine, and Florida. All flew in; no one brought a car. All stayed for three days in the same gangster hotel. All took meals at a very unpretentious but exceptionally good neighborhood restaurant across the street, a surprise we hadn't counted on. All encountered one another and lingered talking in the hotel lobby. All walked the neighborhood sidewalks together, took the nearby el together, visited museums together, and went shopping together. All of which meant that by the time the wedding occurred, *we knew one another*. It wasn't two sets of strangers who mingled briefly and then separated. There was a collective wedding party ready to give our support to the union of two people we knew and loved. The sense of community built during those two days of interaction, a factor no one had foreseen, was the second-finest outcome of the wedding.

Sunny day, beautiful fall weather. We arrived as soon as the gates opened to try to stake out our territory in right field. The usher in charge of our bleacher section was a huge, sturdy fellow named Andre, the kind of person we definitely wanted on our side. Andre had never heard of such a crazy stunt at a baseball game, but he thought it was great. I wondered if lawyer Andy, a master at realizing whom he needs to recruit, had not slipped Andre a one hundred dollar bill.

Andre asked how much space we wanted. "This area right here," we told him.

"Fine," he said. "You got it."

"Should we tape it off?" we asked.

"You don't need to tape it off," Andre said.

"We don't?"

"Naw, I just won't let anybody else sit there." I realized: even among Wrigley's bleacher bums, Andre conveyed no reason whatever to doubt his capacity for imperial rule. He pulled it off effortlessly. In the picture album from the wedding, there is a shot of huge, grinning Andre holding aloft a sign that proclaims, "Go, Andy and Misti, 9/9/99." I more and more suspected that one hundred dollar bill.

As game time approached, the wedding party gathered. The six groomsmen, at Andy's specification, were attired in white shirts, black ties, cummerbunds, and tuxedo jackets. Below the waist, they wore variously colored shorts and Chuck Taylors (retro Converse tennis shoes). Each groomsman wore a bright blue Cub hat. Andy and best man Will (Andy's brother) were dressed the same way.

I had friends back in Louisville, Gwynne and Grover Potts, who were avid Cub fans, attending games whenever they could.

They were not able to be there on the wedding day, but they nevertheless provided a marvelous symbol of their presence in spirit. They had presented me with a "pastoral robe," an extra-extra long Cub shirt that extended nearly to my knees. The back of the shirt provided the wedding benediction. As the ceremony ended, I would turn around and let the gathering view the large word GRACE across my back. Mark Grace was the Cub first baseman, and this was his shirt replica. I also wore a white clerical collar and, of course, a Cub hat.

A few minutes before wedding time, I had gone to the concession stand to get a drink. "Somebody's getting married," had become the common talk across the bleacher as people were realizing the meaning of the unusual outfits. Three guys stopped me as I left the concession area. "Hey, man, are you the Father, that collar and all?"

"I am the pastor."

"Are you serious? Is this for real?"

"Totally for real."

"You're an actual priest, and you're going to hold a wedding here in the bleachers?"

"You got it. Fifteen minutes from now."

"Oh man, I want to join your church."

Younger brother Will, besides being a computer wizard, was also a musician, in rock bands as a percussionist and in bluegrass bands as a banjo player. As his contribution to Andy's big day, Will had composed a wedding song. To the tune of "Take Me Out to the Ballgame" he had written:

> Take the hand of the bride now,
> take the hand of the groom.
> Marry each other and stay that way,
> cherish each other on into your tombs.
> Oh, it's root, root, root for the Chathams,
> if they should part it's a shame,
> for it's one, two, three times *I do*
> at the old ball game.

To the tune of "Daisy, Daisy," Nancy and I had written,

> Misti, Misti, give me your answer true.
> I'm half batty all for the love of you.
> It won't be a stylish wedding.
> Right field will be the setting.
> But you'll look sweet,
> in your bleacher seat,
> as you cheerfully say I do.
>
> Andy, Andy, tell us it's really true.
> Right field bleachers, is that what you want to do?
> What a weird way to start a marriage,
> but let us not disparage.
> Somehow it fits
> your quirky wit,
> so stand up and say *I do*."

Song copies were passed out all through the bleachers by Will and the groomsmen who explained that everyone was to sing on signal. When the time came, Will stood at the foot of Andre's aisle, raised his arms and led the entire bleacher section in a rousing chorus. Even before the game started, some of the patrons were well into the bleacher mood, having packed away enough beer to begin setting aside their normal inhibitions. They belted out the wedding songs, echoing them across the ballpark. It was not enough to get the television cameras focused our way, but it was more than enough to cue the rest of the stadium that a special moment was developing in right field.

The line-ups were announced from the public address system. To a rousing cheer, the Cubs took the field. Everyone stood for the national anthem. As another cheer burst forth at the anthem's end, Misti appeared at the top of the bleacher aisle. She wore a stunning white dress, offset by her long, glistening, strawberry blonde hair, and she carried a bouquet of flowers. It was at this moment that right fielder Sammy Sosa turned, saw what was happening, raised his hat in a celebratory wave, and gave recognition to his corner of

Wrigley. How many of us can say that Sammy Sosa attended our wedding?

Misti proceeded very carefully down the steep bleacher steps. Cheers rained from all around. At the bottom, someone handed her a white veil sewn into a Cub hat. She fitted it on. Then she joined Andy facing me (my back was to the playing field), and I proceeded through the wedding service.

We arrived at the vows.

"Misti, I promise, with God's help, to be your faithful husband, to love and honor you, as Christ commands, as long as we both shall live."

"Andy, I promise, with God's help, to be your faithful wife, to love and honor you, as Christ commands, as long as we both shall live."

Rings were exchanged, and I declared the holy union, "Andy and Misti, according to the will of God, according to the witness of the church of Jesus Christ, and according to the laws of the State of Illinois, I declare that you are now husband and wife." At that moment, I turned to face the baseball field so that the large word *grace* appeared on my back. There was hugging, kissing, and a huge cheer. Congratulations, best wishes, and handshakes passed all around. The wedding had transcended all our hopes. It became one of those mystical days when I just sat there feeling *good* all over, a reflection of the "good" for which Genesis 1 says we were all created.

Does God attend Cub games? I have to acknowledge that I felt very strange saying the marriage liturgy amid the hubbub of right field mania. And yet, if we are to believe the Bible, God has appeared in far more unlikely places: in an Egyptian prison and slave labor camp, in a Jericho whorehouse, amid prisoners of war trekking across the desert, in a fishing boat during the morning catch, in a busy market square filled with townspeople, in a city council meeting rent with controversy. God came to earth through a Galilean peasant boy who lived not as revered royalty in the palaces of the wealthy but as a servant in the huts and hovels of the lowly. He was scorned by authority, derided by those in control. He died by capital punishment because both religion and state suspected him of being a terrorist. After his resurrection, he took up residence not in one of earth's royal domains to wield power and dominion but among the groveling, struggling masses of Galilee to inspire love and justice. After all these things, I have to think that God found Wrigley Field more compatible than some of the super-lavish displays of extravagance where we have traditionally asked the Holy One to show up.

The Cubs came out very lively that day, looking like winners. They scored three runs in the first two innings and seemed poised for more. But, alas, in the middle innings they sagged into normalcy, and Cincinnati won the game five to three. We had picked a typical Wrigley Field day.

During the fourth inning, with all of us talking and enjoying the game, Andy began absentmindedly fidgeting with his newly placed wedding band. It occurred to him to read what Misti had inscribed on the inside. Expecting it to say, "M.L.B. and A.M.C. 9/9/99," he peered into the inner curvature of the ring. He erupted in laughter! He read aloud what Misti had engraved: "Put it back on." From that moment, I knew that, even married to our hyperimaginative son, Misti could take care of herself.

Misti is now the first female partner in a Dallas, Texas, law firm that specializes in construction law. Andy is the Judge of the 282nd Judicial District Court in Dallas.

4

Against Great Odds

ANN WAS a sweet girl, seventeen, not talented at anything in particular, but friendly and pleasant. And eight months pregnant. Grandmother would teach her how to take care of the new child, but Ann still had plenty of child left in her.

Vincent was eighteen, a recent high school graduate with no job, a follower more than a leader, sometimes moody, definitely more suited at this point for shooting baskets on the playground than for fatherhood.

They had both grown up in Eleventh Street Bottom, the former Reynolds Tobacco Company labor village, now a decaying slum, the worst inner-city neighborhood in Winston-Salem. They were taking on all the adult responsibilities with none of the adult resources, except for Ann's grandmother.

I searched my mind to find anything I liked about this union. What chance did it have? What hope was there for the child? Would anyone's future be better?

And yet, I had consented to marry them for several reasons. First, I liked them. Vincent had a quiet earnestness that made me want to believe in him. He might turn out to be pure sham, but there could also be a deeper virtue. Ann bore a natural radiance, a glow that was easy to enjoy. She spent most of her life smiling, outwardly and within.

Performing their marriage would give me one-on-one time with each of them, the opportunity to ask questions about who they were and the kinds of adults they wanted to become. We could talk about married life, the responsibilities of parenthood, work, and education. We could discuss a vision of where all this could lead if they devoted themselves. No results were guaranteed, but I could hope to plant a seed.

And, further, they had asked me. All else aside, that was an honor. It was still the era when a straight-edged, honky preacher could be welcomed in a low income Afro ghetto, but I was sensing that that era was fast vanishing. I was gaining a new cultural education from knowing people like Ann and Vincent, and I felt privileged.

Seventy years earlier, the tobacco company had built Eleventh Street Bottom to house black labor recruited from the Carolinas and Georgia. Cigarette popularity was huge, and Camels were at the top. It was a labor-intensive industry. Machines were used in the assembly lines, but much of the work was done by humans. The tasks were low-skill, easy-to-train-for. People by the hundreds had answered the recruiter's call, migrating to the city for the steady, dependable paycheck.

The Company had thrown up cheap, clapboard housing as fast as it could saw the lumber. Many houses were classic "shotgun," meaning three rooms front to back. The saying was that you could shoot a shotgun in the front door and out the back without hitting anything. Some houses were four-room squares, and a few had a fifth room hanging off the back. A generation later, the company, not wanting to stay in real estate, had sold the houses to private speculators, now labeled "slumlords." There had been virtually no property upkeep in the seven decades since that time. The City paid scant attention to Eleventh Street Bottom, not even enforcing its minimum housing code there. Only when the Federal Government invested massive money into rehabilitating America's inner cities would conditions improve. Ann and Vincent were a pair of kids born too early for that benefit.

Their marriage would take place in a Lutheran church on top of a hill above The Bottom. Pastor Shamburger had told them they were welcome to use his church at no charge. It was awfully good of him; he could easily have said no. Ann and Vincent liked the location.

One of the proudest features of teenage life in The Bottom was something lovingly referred to as "my wardrobe," the collection of good-looking clothes a kid had been able to gather. I heard a lot about their wardrobes but rarely saw the evidence. Most of the time they wore beat-up jeans and sloppy tops. Wedding day was my introduction into the sparkling world of teenage ghetto fashion. The houses these kids lived in might be bedraggled and slummy, but, wow, could they dress! I knew them all, but hardly recognized several, sharp, sleek, and sexy as they had prepared themselves. Vincent wore a suit and tie that befitted a Sunday preacher. Ann, bulging obtrusively, wore a straight dress with ruffled neck, solid black. I wanted to imagine that black symbolized for her the same fresh-beginning purity that the opposite color would have symbolized for a white bride.

We held a quick wedding rehearsal in the hour before. In honor of their two friends, everyone present was intent on "getting it right." I had never before enjoyed such authority. The wedding itself used a formal liturgy, entirely suitable for high-steeple worship. An undercurrent of giggling ran through the whole proceeding, however. These normally cool, suave teenagers were nervous and self-conscious, and this was definitely not familiar territory. As she proceeded down the middle aisle, Ann kept shooting sidewise glances at her friends, giggling all the way. She was straight and erect, however, carrying her baby with innate dignity. We proceeded through the wedding service. "I declare you husband and wife," I said at the end and spoke a benediction. The room flooded in cheers and tears, hugs and kisses. More than just the marriage of

Ann and Vincent, I realized, this event was a declaration of ghetto dignity, a picture of how regally we could act when we set ourselves to do it. These teenagers, long put down and disparaged by the rest of the city, took a quiet pride in seeing themselves as the social equal of anyone else in town. They might not own the finest, but they could muster an impressive event. I was proud of them and glad to have been a part of it.

Someone had prepared a reception, enough nibbles for everyone to eat and talk. Toward the end, I eased over to Vincent and handed him an envelope. My church had put down advance payment for a night for him and Ann in a downtown hotel, and also for their dinner and breakfast in the hotel restaurant. He told me we didn't need to do that. I told him that, helpful as she is, grandma's house is no place for a newly married couple to spend their wedding night. He smiled and accepted gratefully.

Ann's and Vincent's baby is now forty-five years old. I wish I knew the story. Or do I?

5

Expecting the Unexpected

I HAD one suspicion about this wedding. The groom was a magician, a good one, and the wedding was at his house. Which meant that *something* would happen. No guessing what.

Harold was young, late twenties. I knew him, liked him, but when he asked if I would perform his wedding, I had this one reservation. I usually was on top of what would happen at weddings. Not here.

When my younger son was ten years old, he had assembled several magic tricks into a show he performed at nursing homes and kids' birthday parties. In time, he joined the local magic club, a collection of mostly hobbyists and a few professionals who liked to compare antics. We had met Harold in the club. He worked a day job, but in the evenings he did table magic in downtown restaurants. He was a crackerjack! Not on a par with the two young men that club would send to Las Vegas for long entertainment careers, Lance Burton and Mac King, but still *pretty good*! I, who had picked up a lot of magic knowledge transporting my son to perform his shows, sat amazed and completely fooled through Harold's performances.

The wedding occurred on a Saturday afternoon in Harold's living room. The gathering was very pleasant with families and friends from both sides, probably eighteen people. We milled about at first, meeting one another and munching from the huge food layout on the dining room table. "What will Harold do?" a voice inside me kept asking. "Will the wedding cake instantaneously turn into a bouquet of flowers? Will a mysterious voice speak from some faraway region? Will he levitate himself to be as tall as I am? Will he cause the marriage license to vanish and then reappear in my hip pocket?"

We packed into the living room. I stood in front of the fireplace facing outward (summer, no fire). The bride and groom faced me with the best man and maid of honor flanking, All others gathered close, standing. I took us through a fairly simple but nice marriage service. Well along, it occurred to me that Harold didn't have much time left. I looked into his face but found only a magician's innocence. I shouldn't have doubted.

"Do you?"

"I do."

"Do you?"

"I do."

From somewhere below us, there was a sudden flutter. A small bird flew up and landed on Harold's shoulder. Harold looked at the bird; the bird looked at Harold. "Do you approve, Sherlock?" Harold asked. Sherlock nodded vigorously and gave out an affirming squawk. "Good boy," Harold said. "I love your taste." Sherlock squawked again.

"Love is patient and kind. Love is not jealous or boastful. It is not arrogant or rude. Love does not insist on its own way." I continued on through 1 Corinthians 13.

"According to the will of God and according to the laws of the State of Kentucky, I declare that you are now husband and wife." The bird looked at me and nodded again. A musical "cheep" provided his closing commentary. There was a cheer. Sherlock fluttered, arose, and circled three times over our heads before diving back into whatever secret hiding place he had emerged from. I had had fly-overs at funerals, but never before at a wedding.

6

Fifty-One/Forty-Nine

T HE PAIRING did not feel good to me.

Betsy was a twenty-four-year-old member of my church, spirited, vibrant, articulate, and talented. Out of college, she had gone to work with a public relations firm, learning to help clients assess their advertising needs and create programs that would most benefit them. She was a self-confident young woman with poise and humor.

Betsy had become engaged to Matthew. He seemed like a nice guy, a business functionary in mid-level hospital management, possessed with a laughing, sometimes drawling personality. His humor nearly kept up with hers, but beyond that she was in her own category. She would quickly outdistance him in intelligence and accomplishment.

But, Matthew's biggest problem lay elsewhere. He was a proud parishioner in his neighborhood mega-church. He was in training to become an officer in that church, and he talked proudly of how much it meant to him. I knew that his congregation interpreted the Bible literally (in its own manner), and that one of its core beliefs was that women should submit to the authority of their husbands in marriage. The church's preacher was on the radio every Sunday morning as I drove to work, and, while marveling at his superior talents in oral communication, I often objected strongly to what he said, especially regarding women. *She* was supposed to think of *him* as superior, wise, divinely guided, and at the top of their family hierarchy. There was to be no serious challenge, only submission, because that's what the Bible said. My mind ached over Betsy's marrying into that. She was too able a woman.

In our consultation, the three of us had a pleasant conversation. We talked about their identities and their future together. We talked about their families, about roles they expected to play in family life before and after the arrival of children, and about their religious commitments. We talked about conflict and recovery. Matthew, several times, referred to "how God wants our marriage to be." I realized that he had definite ideas that were important to him. He seemed likeable and fun, but he quickly resorted to humor to avoid things he didn't want to talk about. I would move us toward a subject, and he would drop in a triviality for us to laugh at. I was not enchanted.

After an hour, I decided to go straight at what I wanted to know, and wanted her to know. "Matthew, give me the clearest picture you can of how you think God wants the two of you to make difficult decisions in your marriage. When you and Betsy disagree on something, how does God want you to settle it?"

Matthew hesitated. He realized that I knew he had a problem. If he said what his church was teaching him, it could well cause serious stress with Betsy. If he didn't say what his church was teaching him, he would not be telling the truth, which was not his way. He also saw that I wasn't going to let him get away with any more deflection-by-humor.

Betsy grew very quiet.

Matthew finally spoke. "I'd say that in virtually everything, God wants us to share our decisions fifty-fifty. She has a voice, I have a voice, and we will work out things together. On the rare occasions when that doesn't work, I guess it will be fifty-one/forty-nine, just enough to move things forward. I don't think it will happen often, but I think that's God's will for us."

I said, "And she gets the fifty-one, is that right?"

Matthew laughed nervously, not sure where that left us. Betsy didn't laugh at all. I waited to see if she would say anything. She did not.

Should I have pursued it? This is a delicate and difficult moment for a pastor, when red flags appear in pre-marriage consultation. Given the blindness created by fresh love, I can sometimes see things they don't. But should I speak? This couple wasn't asking for my opinion. They had already decided to get married. "Tread lightly where you aren't invited," I reminded myself. I did not speak further.

Six weeks later, I led their marriage. It was happy and joyous. Any cause for hesitation remained well hidden. We sent them off toward a bright and hopeful future.

A formidable hazard in marriage occurs when the man quietly but fundamentally believes that *marriage gives him authority over her*. It does not happen most of the time, but it does happen. "I am the dominant and stronger one, the head-of-household. I earn most of the money, and I should make the final decisions." Nowhere does this apply more critically than regarding sex: "She is supposed to provide when I want." A tabloid headline some years ago read, "Woman bears thirty-two children and then sterilizes husband in his sleep." The Apostle Paul, in seeking to bring order and civility to a conflicted church in Ephesus, had no idea the mischief he was unleashing on future generations when he wrote, "Wives, be subject to your husbands as you are to the Lord." (Eph 5:22). Literal biblical interpretation creates from this a God-ordained power hierarchy.

Yes, there are some women who profess that they *want* this kind of marriage relationship, that they wish for a strong male figure who will guide them in right paths. Many more women don't buy a word of that, knowing that the quest for the best way needs to be a joint venture.

Before marriage, the man and woman are trying so hard to please each other that any domineering tendency in him goes underground. In time, things change, however, sometimes shockingly. It can be a heartbreaking and frightful experience for her. ("How did I get into this tyrannical relationship, and will it happen again the next time? Are all men like this?").

After four years with Matthew, Betsy was gone. His presumed authority, his suspicion of her, and his jealousy were too much. Matthew's church supported him, assuring him that he was following God's will, that she was the one who needed to shape up. Self-certain religion can inflict huge damage.

7

Get Me to the Church on Time

H E WAS a musician, she an artist. They specialized in effect, not logistics.

The wedding guests sat in place, a hundred people gathered to share this joyous moment. The organist played Pachabel's "Canon," Bach's "That Sheep May Safely Graze," and other classical selections. The flower arrangements were beautiful, tasteful sprays of color. The candles were lit, brightly glowing. The grandparents, aunts, uncles, cousins, and parents were seated. The groomsmen were ready in the back room, the bridesmaids in a rear foyer. The seven-year-old flower girl delicately examined the flower petals with her small fingers, and the even younger ring bearer wiggled the two pillow pins in patterns to amuse himself. The photographer stood at the foot of the entry aisle ready to snap the women as they came down. I signaled the organist, "Keep playing! Not ready!"

We had one major problem: no groom. Seven o'clock. was the appointed time, and it was now 7:06: no groom. Late to your own wedding! Caught in traffic? Car broken down? Hurt and bleeding by the roadside? Half dead in a hospital? Last minute crush of necessities? Cold feet? Where is he?

He's setting himself up for a lifetime of ridicule! From family and friends, he would be hearing about this with juicy elaboration into the third and fourth generations. To mark yourself indelibly, there is no better way than to be late to your own wedding. "You fool, what are you doing to yourself?"

At 7:13, the door opened. He loped in, looking rushed and disheveled, tie slightly twisted, hair out of place, forehead perspiring, collar askew. But he was there! And quickly repairable. A little water, a towel, and a mirror, and we could have him moving. Slightly embarrassing, but it could have been much worse. The organist, as always, had a large stack of music, well prepared for delay. He was *really good*, and no one regretted the concert.

I was standing there thinking how livid the bride must be, knotted with anxiety. *"George, how could you? Our special day!"* I sent a runner to the back of the sanctuary to alert the women that we were ready.

But the runner returned with another problem: no bride. She hadn't arrived yet either. Everyone had assumed she would come fully dressed and ready, but as of this moment she had not arrived at all. "My God, is this real?" I thought. More music. "Am I ever glad for how good that organist is!"

At 7:25, she sauntered in. Nothing unusual. She took a few minutes for final preparations, and the wedding began at 7:40. It was beautiful.

The revealing factor was that no one was surprised. "Oh, that's just George and Linda," said friends and family. I realized that all the hang-ups were in me. Someday I'll learn.

8

Nightmare Day

TWICE IN thirty-eight years I became really angry at a wedding. One of those stories is enough. Here it is.

They had seemed like a pleasant young couple. He worked in an office downtown; she was finishing her master's degree at the university. They were not members of our church, and I don't remember why I was marrying them. I usually confined myself to church members and personal friends.

I had met with the couple two or three times to do pre-marriage counseling and to work out the type of wedding they wanted. They had expressed the wish to have their reception in the church fellowship room after the wedding, not in another location as most couples did. They had made that choice because of convenience, and probably also because renting our fellowship room was a lot cheaper than renting a downtown social club.

I had given them a copy of our wedding guidebook. I had walked through it with them to make sure they took in the essentials. The church had a zero-alcohol policy, causing many couples to go elsewhere. We weren't anti-alcohol. Plenty of our members drank, but we did not have the staff to oversee alcohol events in the building. Also, some of our members were recovering alcoholics. We knew the struggle they were involved in and did not want their church offering them temptation.

Four days before the wedding, I arrived at work in the morning and was greeted by the church bookkeeper. "Jim, I wish you had been here yesterday afternoon. Two women involved in Saturday's wedding came through here like a hurricane, demanding that we all abandon everything we were doing and become their servants. They wanted us to show them the sanctuary, show them the fellowship room, show them the kitchen and what's in it, show them the candelabras and the flower containers, show them the table cloths, show them the reception tables. They were upset that there is no center aisle in the sanctuary and wanted us to explain how a wedding can be held under conditions like that. They stormed through here like they owned us. I called Mack (the head maintenance man), and the last I saw, Mack, in his patient, calm way, was enduring their ranting. Who are these people?"

I phoned the bride and asked if the women who had been in the afternoon before had seen the wedding guidebook, that there seemed to be some misunderstandings. She assured me that everything was okay now, that all the questions had been worked out. I believed her and hoped that would settle it.

Wedding day came. I went by my office in the morning dressed in jeans and a polo shirt. Hearing noises in the sanctuary, I went out to see what was happening. To my surprise, I found that the pulpit had been dismantled and converted into a flower stand, meaning that as I stood to marry the couple, a large vase of flowers would be growing out the top of my head. Three men and two women were discussing how to push the grand piano up one of the inclined sanctuary aisles to the back. I intervened. "I'm sorry, friends, but the pulpit remains a pulpit, and the piano stays where it is."

"That can't be," scowled one woman. I realized I had just met one of our earlier antagonists. "This piano doesn't belong in here for a wedding. No one is playing it, it's in the way, and we have to get rid of it. And there's no reason at all to have a pulpit there. It dominates everything, and we need the space for flowers."

"There's one very good reason. This is a worship sanctuary, and the pulpit is central to worship. We don't do away with it. As for the piano, pushing it around will de-tune it, and the church needs it for tomorrow morning's worship. The piano stays where it is."

"But we're having a wedding in here this afternoon, not worship."

"A wedding is worship, ma'am."

She nearly exploded! "We rented this space, and we can do what we want with it! Who are you telling us what we can and can't do?"

"I'm the pastor, and I'll be leading the wedding, ma'am."

Her cohorts were quickly backing off. But the woman herself was unrelenting. "How were we supposed to know this? Why didn't you tell us before we did all this work? This is outrageous!"

"Have you read the church's wedding guidebook?" I asked.

"What wedding guidebook? I haven't seen any wedding guidebook."

"The one I gave the bride and groom two months ago."

"Well, it never reached me!"

"I'm sorry for that. It tells everything I'm telling you now."

Her friends were reassembling the pulpit. Little did I know that this was just the beginning.

I arrived an hour early for the five o'clock wedding. Our second-in-command custodian, Bob, was on duty, and the entire place was at its loveliest. Things seemed to be going well until I saw cardboard boxes labeled "Gallo," "Rothschild," and "Beringer" being loaded into the fellowship room.

I went immediately to the groom. "Alcohol is not allowed at receptions here. What are these boxes that are coming in the door?"

"It's only wine," he replied. "We thought that would be okay."

"It's not okay. The church does not allow alcohol events in the building. I don't know how we could have said it more clearly."

"Well, we've already bought the wine for the reception, and it's loaded in and ready to go."

Okay, quick decision time for me. We are forty-five minutes before the wedding. Do I stick with the church's rule? I could dictate that the boxes stay sealed, and I knew what kind of mood that would create. Or do I proceed forward and hope for no bad results? Most alcohol receptions go perfectly well. Old cream puff me, I took the latter choice.

With around two hundred guests ushered in and the families seated, I assembled the groomsmen and groom. Of six grooms-men, five were men in their twenties and thirties and one, the bride's little brother, was about eleven. We lined up by the entry door. When the time came, I looked behind me and said, "Here we go." In that moment, I became aware that a sizable bottle of Maker's Mark bourbon had just passed mouth-to-mouth down the line and was nearly empty at the far end. Maker's Mark is power-ful stuff, a great bourbon but more like battery acid when drunk straight. The eleven-year-old stood at the far end of the line hold-ing the empty bottle with a perplexed, "What am I supposed to do with this?" look on his face. Instead of opening the sanctuary door, I opened the organ loft door and signaled for the organist to keep playing. I then stepped back and took the bottle from the young man, putting it in a trash can. I found a messenger to send around to the women, "There will be a short delay." I returned to the groomsmen. Most of them seemed okay; one looked blurry. I took him to a chair and sat him down. I sent someone for food, any kind of food. The runner came back with a plate of crackers and cheese. "Eat," I said. He looked at me. "We're not going out there until you eat something. Eat!" He ate two crackers with cheese. We had to get him a cup of water. "Eat more." Three or four crackers-and-cheeses later, I let him stop. I passed the remains among the others. We waited several minutes. I had been through this scene before, once having to prop a best man in a chair to keep him ver-tical. We were not going to have one of these guys pass out on the sanctuary floor, disrupting a beautiful wedding, causing him to have to be carried out, and leaving everyone annoyed and disgusted. We would wait.

A messenger came from the women: "What's wrong, and how long?" Message back: "Nothing prohibitive, five minutes." We sat until the worst-off groomsman seemed to collect himself. I stood him up; he looked stable. "Everybody else okay?" They all nodded. I sent a messenger to the women that we were ready, lined up the men, signaled the organist, and we proceeded into the sanctuary. I was holding my breath. At least they were going to stand alongside the grand piano which could steady them if necessary. That piano might play a role in this wedding after all. The women joined us at the front, and a quick check revealed that the men appeared vertical and stable.

"Blessed be God the Creator," I began, "who gave the planets their orbits and the stars their appointed rhythms, who created time and space and history." I began weddings by giving thanks that the God who had created the entire cosmos was also creating this marriage. With those words, I sensed an unexpected movement beyond my right shoulder. Surprised, I turned to look. No more than five feet from my face was an absurd sight: from between two flower stands, both adorned with large bouquets, had popped a jack-in-the-box photographer with his camera held aloft. He was trying to get close into the inner circle. His flash camera was aimed directly at my eyes. It's a good thing he did not flash it because I would probably have decked him. I had once previously had a flash set off directly in my eyes, and the effect was mind-numbing pain. He lowered his camera and stared at me with an Alfred E. Newman grin. I laughed, derisively. Then, I bored into him a look that would have withered an oak tree. I reached down and switched off my microphone. "Get the *hell* out of here!" I said softly. He heard me. He withered back into the flower arrangement and did not re-emerge. I knew by then that this couple had paid *no* attention to the church's wedding manual.

We carried through to the end of the service uneventfully. I was smiling joyfully as if this were the happiest Saturday afternoon of my life, feeling very differently inside. When the wedding was over and pictures had been posed, I bid everyone my best wishes and headed home. The reception would be under the supervision of our custodian, Bob.

But something didn't feel right. I was uneasy. I changed clothes, slid back into the car, and returned to the church.

I walked into the fellowship room and was greeted by Bob. "Jiiiimm, I liiiike this kinda weddin! Weee oughta dooo weddins like this moooe ofen!" Bob's voice slurred, his eyes swimming.

"Oh, my God. Don't tell me they invited you into the booze!" Bob was an able, dependable, honest, wonderful guy, except on the periodic occasions when he got drunk and quickly became worthless. Not thirty minutes into the reception, and Bob had found it. "Theeese are reeeaal niiiice people, Jiiiimm. I liiike thiiis group." I couldn't believe what I was seeing.

"Bob, where is your truck key?"

"Riiight heeere, Jiiimm,"

"Give it to me." Bob handed it over. I dipped into my pocket and pulled out four quarters. "Okay, Bob, take these quarters, walk up to the bus stop, get on the bus, bury yourself in a seat, don't talk to anybody, stay apart, ride home, go inside, lock your doors, put yourself to bed, and go to sleep. You're scheduled to work here tomorrow morning, and we need you. The last thing I want is for you to get arrested for public drunkenness or D.U.I. I'll give you your truck key back in the morning. The truck will be fine in the church parking lot until then."

"Buuut, Jiiimm, whoooo wiiill clooose down the building after the weddin?"

"I will!"

"Jiiimm!"

"Bob, *go!*" Bob went. He knew he wasn't fired. He was too valuable, and we had too good a relationship for that. But he also knew that I was not the least bit enchanted over how my Saturday evening was going to be spent. The wedding party would have already paid for him to receive a healthy overtime honorarium, and I would leave him wondering whether he would receive it all, which he did.

The reception was going well. Conversations dotted the room. Alcohol was prominently present but not obtrusive. In my mind, however, I contrasted the scene this night with the one the night before in this same room when two hundred struggling souls had gathered in their life-or-death attempt to escape the thing this group was imbibing liberally. I hoped that no one from Alcoholics Anonymous would show up on the wrong night.

After a few minutes, I heard the next chapter in the evening's saga. "Plink! Plink! Plink! Plink!" Loud percussion sounds came down the steps from the floor above. Somebody was creating a concert. I knew immediately what was happening, and I motored myself up the stairs.

The church's children's choir director had purchased a very nice set of orph instruments to use in accompanying the choir. They were expensive enough that she stored them in a locked closet in the choir room. Two members of the wedding party, both well lubricated, had pried the lock off and spread out the orph instruments across the room. They were gleefully bouncing about, banging on this one, banging on that one, as if the delicate little devices were base drums. They had already worked out a high-volume rendering of "Mary Had a Little Lamb," and they were headed into "Row, Row, Row Your Boat." Each was trying to out-noise the other. The instruments were straining beneath the beating.

"Stop it!" I roared, as I entered the room.

They looked up, surprised. "Oh, Mr. Killjoy."

"These are children's instruments, not made to be banged on by adults. You're going to destroy them."

"We're just having a little fun, not hurting anything."

"The concert is over! Get out of here! You're supposed to be down in the reception room, not roaming the church halls seeing what kind of little fun you can have. You are to exit this room *now*, not later!" I was non-negotiable.

"Aw, man, these are neat. We'll play for just a little bit. We went to a lot of trouble to get them out. Don't make us put them up."

"Leave! Now! No more! Finished! Through! You're gone! Out of here!"

The message finally penetrated their clouded heads. "Aw, man, a bummer." They stumbled to comply.

I returned downstairs and once again went to the groom. "Two drunken members of the wedding party have been upstairs banging on the children's orph instruments which they pulled out of a locked closet. I suggest you go up there and make sure everything is put back in good order and that your friends stay away. Those instruments are not cheap. If they are destroyed, they will triple your bill for using this church." He, looking very remorseful, grabbed a nearby friend and went. By now, I was seething, just wanting to get this wretched event over.

Then, there was a new noise. Crash-shatter! Crash-shatter! Crash-shatter! The noise came from outside the building. "What in the world?" I dashed through the hallway, down the steps, and out into the cobblestone alley behind the church. The reception was winding down, and the bride had commissioned three young men to carry cases of empty wine bottles out to the trash cans for disposal. The young men had decided to turn the bottle disposal into a game. They had lined up three open trash cans against the brick building side, backed up several paces, and vied to see who could land the largest number of wine bottles in the trash cans. They were throwing so hard that the bottles were crashing against the brick and shattering in every direction. Fifteen bottles must have been hurled by the time I got there.

"Stop it, you idiots!" I shouted. "Don't you have any common sense? Neighborhood cars drive up and down this alley, and you have just riddled several dozen tires with broken glass! You are to set those bottles one-by-one in the trash cans. Then you are to pick up every shard of broken glass in this alley. We're not leaving tonight until this place is spotless! You may as well get at it." I was furious.

"Man, we're at a party. Didn't they pay to use this place?"

"You spoiled jerk! Have you grown up with somebody else always cleaning up behind you? New revelation: *I Am not your servant!* You're not going to trash this building and then walk away. These neighbors may not be your friends, but they are ours. Clean it up, now! And make sure nobody drives through here before you finish!"

Again, I found the groom. "Several young men have been out back shattering wine bottles against the church building, splattering broken glass all over our back alley. Neighborhood cars use that alley regularly. It has to be clean before we leave here this evening. I suggest you round up several wedding guests and get started. It's a mess!"

He rolled his eyes. He was beginning to get the point. Within moments, tuxedo-clad wedding guests were on hands and knees in the back alley digging glass shards from around the one hundred-year-old street bricks, illumined by the streetlight overhead. A couple of bridesmaids came out to help. I wished for that photographer now. After thirty minutes, the alley was clean.

Groom and bride thanked me, apologized profusely for the difficulties, and bade me farewell. I told them I wished for them a good life and a supremely happy marriage. We parted friends. I locked the church doors at 10:00 p.m. All I had to do the next morning was teach a class, preach two sermons, and give Bob his truck key back, a flip compared with this night before. I hoped I could get rid of my anger.

9

A Great Cloud of Witnesses

MACK WAS the head of maintenance in our church. A chunky, sturdy, mostly taciturn man of perhaps sixty-three, he was as dependable as the rising sun with a bullish determination for getting things the way he believed they ought to be. I could depend on him to relate well to the many church members he and I worked for, a few of whom could be quirky and demanding. I loved Mack as one of the most indispensable people on the church staff and also as a friend.

Josie worked there also, "housekeeper" being her title. She was supposed to rank under Mack, but for running the kitchen and keeping the church clean, Josie ranked under nobody. The younger maintenance staff learned quickly that they needed to read Josie's face as she snooped across their territory. Josie had a pleasant, likeable personality, but without a word, she could say with clarity, "This place isn't right, and it's *your* job to get it that way *now*!" I loved Josie every bit as much as Mack. When Nancy and I celebrated out fortieth wedding anniversary, Josie occupied a featured seat. Mack had died by then, or he would have been there too.

Josie and Mack informed me one day that they wanted to get married. They would hold their marriage ceremony on a Saturday afternoon in the large back yard of Josie's sister, Molly, and they asked if I could perform the ceremony. I told them I would be highly honored.

On the appointed Saturday, I pulled up at Molly's house about forty-five minutes before wedding time. The party was at full bore. In the front yard talking with friends was Tony, Josie's son, who had worked for the church for a time, but who had had a chronic habit of showing up thirty minutes late and making up for it by leaving thirty minutes early. I also wondered seriously where Tony was making all his money. He sported himself around in a new, gold Chrysler Imperial, certainly not purchased on his church salary. I once had a police officer friend snoop through our inner basement to see if the church had also become a drug store. After I fired Tony, he and I had an uneasy relationship, but we both managed to get through our occasional encounters.

On the front porch was a son of Molly's, Cedric, who would, upon Mack's retirement a few years later, become director of maintenance at the church. Cedric was smart, savvy, very personable, hardworking, and totally dependable. Also prone to touches of jiving and playfulness, he was a fun guy. I treasured Cedric as one of our best-ever employees.

In the living room was another of Molly's sons, John. In the twenty-five years I worked at Highland Presbyterian Church, the church burglar alarm must have gone off a thousand times, summoning one of us staff members, deep in the night, to drive down, turn the alarm off, search the place, and then secure it again. *The only* time there was ever a burglar was the night John, in need of money, found an unlocked window, eased in, and broke into the Coke machine looking for dimes and quarters. If only he had asked me, I would happily have given him the money he needed. He was fundamentally a nice guy, if not very dependable. We had a brief but cheerful conversation on wedding day. On into the house, I met cousins, aunts, uncles, nieces, nephews, and friends. The greetings were cordial and lively.

On the back porch was Molly's daughter, Vanessa. Vanessa had made a career out of providing quality home care to aging people across the city. She was good, and highly sought. Getting on Vanessa's employment calendar was pure luck if a person managed to do it.

One of the teenagers had brought a boom box, and the dance floor had been set up in the old concrete driveway at the back of Molly's property. Six or seven kids were back there dancing to Motown Sound, setting an undertone beat for everyone present. A lot of souls knew what do with that rhythm.

The whole mood was festive, and the snacks were the best Molly and friends knew how to prepare. I didn't smell a drop of alcohol anywhere. Josie had been through family alcoholism in earlier years, and she would have scorched the property dry with a single scowl. *Everybody* knew who the boss was on this day, and everybody knew the rules.

At the appointed hour, I gathered the wedding party in the middle of the back yard and began the ceremony. Call to worship. Invocation. Interpretation of marriage. It was about here that I realized a remarkable thing. Not only had family members and friends clustered close, but outside the yard a crowd was gathering along the fence. Neighbors from their porches and houses on the block, people who had been walking on the sidewalks, the barber and two other gentlemen from the barber shop across the corner, several people from the gas station, two beat cops who had parked their bicycles on the sidewalk, the driver of a Bunny Bread delivery truck, several people who had just gotten off a bus headed home, and folks who had been tidying up a church yard. Elbows lined the fence perimeter, everyone peering in. "Incredible!" I thought to myself. "This whole community knows Mack and Josie, and they have stepped forward to marry two of their finest. This is how marriage ought to happen. It's not just a man and a woman. It's two families, two communities. And the whole aggregation has gathered here this afternoon."

I reached the point in the ceremony when I looked out across the gathering and said, "I ask now for the commitment of everyone here. Do the family and friends of the bride commit yourselves to do everything in your power to uphold and sustain Josie and Mack in their life together? If you do, please say, 'I do.'"

There was a modest mumble, "I do," not nearly enough.

"Let's try that again! If this marriage is to last, we've got to mean what we say. So let's hear it for real! Do the family and friends of the bride, Josie, commit yourselves to do everything in your power to uphold and sustain Josie and Mack in their life together. If you do, and if you really mean it, please *shout*, 'I do!'"

A roar arose from the gathering, "I do!"

"Do the family and friends of the groom, Mack, commit yourselves to do everything in your power to uphold and sustain Josie and Mack in their life together. If you do, and if you really mean it, please *shout*, 'I do!'" A giant thunder erupted, conveying the notion that this entire corner of the city was committing itself to the marriage. Josie stood smiling happily. And Mack, even staid, sturdy, un-expressive Mack, welled up in a slight, dark-eyed tear.

I moved on through the ceremony. When I reached, "According to the will of God, and according to the laws of the state of Kentucky, I declare that you are husband and wife," a celebration broke out. It transformed the proceeding into a collective moment that belonged to everyone. It lifted Josie and Mack on a carpet of support and swept them forward. It announced to the universe that a new creation was happening here, a creation by God filled with promise and hope. It welcomed Josie and Mack into their new world. "That," I thought, "is how marriage ought to be: a collective commitment of everyone!" I went away that day feeling very, very good.

PART TWO

Dispatching

10

A Garland Instead of Ashes[1]

IT IS about 9:30 on an August evening, an hour after dark. I am driving down a sparsely settled road outside the village of Union Church, Mississippi. Cornfields on both sides near their maturity, and soon the stalks will be chopped and dried for winter cattle feeding. The pavement bends sharply right, but I take the dirt road straight ahead. Even my small Volkswagen taillights illuminate the massive cloud of dust behind me.

Passing through a wooded area, my headlights find the two rearview mirrors of a pickup truck parked beside a driveway. I turn into the driveway, and, to my astonishment, find perhaps thirty cars and small trucks parked around the farmyard. A human figure I can not identify, but who has already identified me, motions me into a parking space beside the farmhouse. I pull in and exit the Volkswagen. Small groups of men stand around the farmyard conversing in low tones. Several of them acknowledge me as I reach the front porch.

"What happened?" I inquire. The story unfolds.

Herman Galbreath, forty-eight-years-old, left home shortly after lunch on this Saturday to go to Brookhaven. He had told his wife, Katherine, that he needed to go to the hardware store. But

1. Adapted from Chatham, James O. *Sundays Down South: a Pastor's Stories* (Jackson: University Press of Mississippi, 1999), 72–77.

he must have gone other places too, because when he came driving back down that dirt road at 3:45 in the afternoon, he wasn't handling the wheel entirely steadily.

Amery Rutledge, the Galbreaths' next-door neighbor, came driving down the road behind Herman and watched him as he weaved slightly from side to side. Suddenly Herman stopped, and Amery stopped behind him. Amery blew his horn. In the next moment, 218-pound Herman was advancing on Amery's pickup, fists clenched, eyes flaming, cursing and growling like an angry tiger. Amery, sixty-five pounds smaller, reached for his shotgun. Herman threw the cab door open and saw the gun. He clawed wildly at his neighbor just as Amery fired. Herman slumped to the road, dead.

No charges had been filed and none would be, but everyone in that farmyard is wondering if Amery couldn't have figured out something better to do than what he did.

I pass the yellow bug light by the front door and enter the frame house. Inside, there are women everywhere, wives of the men in the yard. I scan the room quickly to see if Katherine Galbreath is among them, too new in my profession to realize that she will not be. One woman, whose face I recognize, greets me and announces my presence to the room. I am accorded general welcome.

She then leads me to the kitchen which is laid out like an executive smorgasbord: ham, chicken, roast beef, turkey, corn, collards, snaps, potato salad, sliced tomatoes, homemade bread, and about twenty varieties of cakes and pies. She hands me a plate and tells me to help myself. I thank her and decline—my dinner was only thirty minutes before. I have been an ordained pastor only five weeks, and it will be sometime later before I discern that in this situation *you eat*, whether it is noon or midnight, whether you are hungry or not. It is a gesture of respect for people who respect you.

The food has been prepared by those gathered, the friends and neighbors of the bereaved. They have done it many times before, and they will do it many times again. Their instinct is to help in this helpless situation, so that they do the thing they know will at least help some: they bring food. By tomorrow sisters, brothers, cousins, aunts, uncles, nieces, and nephews will begin to gather to comfort the widow, and all of these people will need to be fed. The nearest restaurant is more than twenty miles away, so that the neighbors set up a food line in the widow's kitchen, a sincere expression of their concern. And they stand about the house, the women inside and the men in the yard, no one saying much because there really isn't much to say, and because they don't consider themselves very good at saying things anyway. But all of them saying by their presence that they know the hell this middle-aged farmer's wife is going through because they have all been through it themselves in one form or another, and they don't want her to have to go through it alone. They will all stay until late in the night, well after Katherine Galbreath has gone to bed, and a few of the women will remain until relatives began to arrive the next day. It is a time for human solidarity, not for loneliness, the community at its best.

My hostess shows me to a bedroom where Katherine Galbreath is seated among three friends. As I enter, the friends draw back slightly, expecting me to take the lead, and believing that the widow and I should be accorded privacy if we want it. I greet them and invite the friends to stay.

"It's awfully nice of you to come, Reverend," Katherine says, thoughtfully conveying to me that she regards my arrival as more than just ministerial duty.

"I know this is a difficult time for you, Mrs. Galbreath," I reply. She sobs gently, acknowledging that what I have spoken is true.

"I heard the gunshot," she says "I thought someone must be shooting a crow. I had no idea it was my husband being shot." She breaks down in tears.

'It's horrible," I say. "I feel *so deeply* for you right now."

"Will you please pray with me, Reverend?" she finally asks. I take her hand, and in the touch I feel her pain even more strongly. "Pray with me for some light in this cursed darkness!" she is saying. "Tell God that my head is spiraling through space, that I have no idea how to calm it down, that the life has been wrung from my body and the spirit from my heart! See if this horrid nightmare cannot somehow be canceled, if heaven will not grant a miracle that will return the world to 3:00 o'clock this afternoon and bring Herman safely through that door! Tell God about the misery I am going through and that I doubt I can stand it much longer!" I pray, acknowledging Mrs. Galbreath's deep anguish, asking strength for her, and giving thanks for her family and friends.

"I was thinking just the other day," she says, "how fortunate we were: Roselynn happily married to Johnny Spencer over in Meadville, Katherine Ann doing so well in her last year of high school, and Howard growing up to take over his father's farm someday. Everything seemed perfect. I was very happy. And now this. Why did it have to happen? That's what I keep asking. Why did such a useless little incident have to lead to my husband's death?"

I can not say to her, "It happened because we are all exiles from Eden, fugitives and wanderers on the earth who slay and are slain. It happened because we are all brothers and sisters of Cain, victims of the jealousy by which the first farmer killed his brother. It happened because Lamech lives within us, the spirit of vengeance and retaliation against any who challenge our self-imagined importance." I can not say these things to her, but I need not. She knows them already. She is familiar with that fundamental human instinct, so apparent in this quiet, Bible belt community, to set everything straight by violence. She knows that every pickup truck in Jefferson County, Mississippi, carries a shotgun in the rear window not just to kill buzzards. She has watched neighbor fight with neighbor before and understands what can happen.

Child of the exile, mother of the crucified, wife of the concentration camp victim, widow of the war dead, your voice is one and its sound is everywhere. Your question joins the pleas of people in all ages who have walked the valley of the shadow of a loved one's violent death and cried out, "When, O God, can the killing stop? When will the creation be reborn? When will the wretched horror that seizes our lives and destroys our hearts stalk us no longer?"

In answer to these pleas, God has spoken a promise. God said it long ago, and we have possessed it for a very long time. But the promise is heard compellingly only when our hearts are ready to receive it, by those who can go no further without it, because without the promise there is no reason to go further. That is precisely where Katherine Galbreath is at this moment.

"They shall beat their swords into plowshares, and their spears into pruning hooks; nation shall not lift up sword against nation, neither shall they learn war any more" (Isa 2:4). Men and women shall rest under their vines and under their fig trees. Farmers shall harvest what they plant, and families shall enjoy the cool fall breezes sitting in thatch-backed rocking chairs on their porches watching the grandchildren play in the front yard, and none shall make them afraid. Killing and bloodshed shall afflict them no more, for the mouth of the Lord has spoken!

Are these just the empty dreams of prophetic idealists? Perhaps. Maybe we are foolish to record such poetry in holy writ and teach it to our children. But consider, are there not signs, hidden but unmistakable, of its coming? Look, for instance, at the group assembled around this farmyard at this very moment. Look at the gifts they have brought: gold, frankincense, and myrrh, presented to one who is losing her life as a sure sign that she will regain it? Their act speaks God's promise. Their instinct for human relationship is God's building stone. Their sturdiness is God's supportive strength. Their graciousness God's love. These Mississippi farm people, best known across the nation in this tumultuous year of 1964 as southern rednecks, their presence in Katherine Galbreath's life is God's promise, a veiled but sure sign of the future.

"He will feed his flock like a shepherd; he will gather the lambs in his arms, and carry them in his bosom, and gently lead the mother sheep" (Isa 40:11). This is the word the Lord has spoken, and the ambassadors of the Lord silently proclaim it to all with ears to hear.

"Cry the bitter cries of grief, Katherine Galbreath! Lament your loss and struggle with your difficult future. But know that the time is coming when God will wipe away every tear from your eyes, and mourning, pain, and death shall be no more. Yes, the mouth of the Lord has spoken."

We talk briefly of funeral arrangements. We will bury Herman Galbreath two days later amid a packed congregation at Union Church Presbyterian Church, the first funeral of my pastoral career. Remorse will fill every soul, and all present will vow that this must never happen again, even though we know it will. The unsettled issue running through the funeral will be: can the community ever forgive Amery Rutledge? His was a pathetic solution to a not-that-difficult problem. Can we move beyond what he did? We have to.

Katherine Galbreath thanks me for coming. I press her hand in final empathy. I arise and leave through the same gathering that greeted me. As I drive up the road, I find myself very sad over the pain the Galbreath family must suffer, the difficult future they face. But I also find in me a quiet joy over the sheer beauty of everything I have just seen and heard.

Twenty-four hours later, on Sunday evening, a young eighteen-year-old man, a neighbor of the Galbreaths, will drive his family's pickup truck to the funeral home seventeen miles away to visit at Herman's wake. On his way home, the right-side wheels of his pickup will, as he rounds a turn, slide off the road and down an embankment, flipping the truck. The young man will lie unconscious in a puddle of gasoline for six hours before dying in a hospital on Monday. Upon learning of both these tragedies, an eighty-eight-year-old Union Church man will die of a heart attack. These will be the second and third funerals of my pastoral career. It will be the only time in thirty-eight years that I conduct three funerals in one week.

11

Big Plans and Little People

"You ever meet Mr. Jackson?" Jimmie Pettigrew, my working cohort in East Eleventh Street Bottom, asked. The year was 1971. Jimmie had grown up in the neighborhood and knew everyone. I had worked there only five years and was still learning.

"No, I don't know Mr. Jackson," I replied.

"Cum'on."

Mr. Jackson lived at the southern extremity of The Bottom, at Ninth and Dunleith Streets. He was a handsome, well-preserved, seventy-seven-year-old man. Married earlier in life, his wife had "passed" after an illness. He lived alone in a five-room house similar to others in the neighborhood, except that his had been well cared for through the years. The foundation was sturdy, the siding and windows in good repair, and the roof strong. He had purchased this house long ago. He had built a large screened porch on the front which let him sit outside comfortably on summer nights. He had placed an easy chair on that porch, a radio on a table beside the chair, and two rockers and a swing for visiting neighbors. He had installed a ceiling fan to provide a breeze.

Mr. Jackson exemplified something thoroughly American. From a rural South Carolina farm, he had moved into The Bottom as a very young man to labor in the tobacco factory. He had disciplined himself from his earliest years. His mother had told him,

60

"Remember, son, what you get is what you work for." Her words still lived in him. Laboring at R.J. Reynolds for a decade and a half, he had saved enough money to buy this house. After moving in, he had set to work to create his dream.

There were now five rooms on the house, one of which he had built to accommodate his growing family. He had also attached a carport. He currently owned his second automobile, a 1954 Chevrolet. All this was accomplished on the salary he had earned as a line worker at Reynolds and on his wife's income as a hospital attendant.

In time, Mr. Jackson had saved enough money to purchase two vacant lots next to his house. He had erected a chain-link fence around the entire property. It was then that he embarked on his real love, growing his half-acre garden. He planted corn, snaps, green peas, squash, lettuce, onions, tomatoes, okra, and potatoes. If he couldn't still live on that South Carolina farm, he could import a piece of it into the city. A happier man did not live in The Bottom. He knew what would make him content in life, and he accomplished it. His property was a startling sight. Amid shanties, dirt streets, and piles of refuse was a masterfully crafted garden lush with homegrown delights.

Year after year, Hezekiah Jackson was to be found tilling, planting, fertilizing, weeding, and harvesting, always gathering more than his family could eat. He found great joy in sharing food with his neighbors, a bag of vegetables for Mrs. Cook, potatoes for Mr. Crest, fresh corn for the Miller family, vine-ripened tomatoes for everyone. Mr. Jackson had no impulse to build larger barns to secure himself but only to build community by his unending benevolence. I wished he could have shared that spirit with some in the city who were considerably better off. Why had no church ever asked him to speak?

The early August day when I first visited him found his garden at peak production. He had bags of freshly gathered produce on the front porch ready for delivery up and down the street. He had been harvesting and sorting since the night before. It was obviously a day his neighbors would enjoy.

But Mr. Jackson was not feeling very good. A few days earlier he had received a letter in the mail. The town fathers were announcing that Eleventh Street Bottom had blighted the east end of the city long enough. City government had moved proactively to take advantage of Federal Urban Renewal money. The Bottom was to be leveled, all its current dwellings demolished. It was to be rebuilt with modern housing, townhouses to accommodate younger residents and high rises to care for the elderly. The entire area, three-tenths of a square mile, home to four thousand people, would become a fresh, new, state-of-the-art neighborhood. A housing authority worker would visit him soon to consult about his particular future.

Mr. Jackson had read these sparkling words, but through them he heard something very different: no more fresh corn off the stalk, no more vine-ripened tomatoes, no more tender baby squash, no more soaking the dirt off newly dug potatoes, no more sharing with neighbors, no more front porch to sit on, no more five-room house of his own making. His entire life was about to vanish. The City had concocted a big plan, benevolent, worthwhile, long overdue. But Mr. Jackson knew how big plans can annihilate little people, like himself. He knew he had no hope against the powers of Government.

A few weeks later, a worker came to see Mr. Jackson. He showed her his accomplishments, his farm in the inner city. Her response was that urban renewal would be a grand and wonderful thing for everyone, that even though his property would have to be leveled, he would be well taken care of. She told him he could have a new garden (it turned out to be six-by-ten feet) where he could plant and harvest. She said he would be given the choice of whether he wanted to live higher or lower in the elderly highrise—the view from up high would be marvelous.

The central message through the entire interview was, "We will take good care of you. This is for your benefit." The unspoken, underlying message was, "You should be grateful to us. We are doing you a huge favor." Spoken to a man who had spent his life perfectly well taking care of himself in his own way, this was a bitter message.

I saw Mr. Jackson several more times, once when we tried to negotiate a better solution in the Urban Renewal office. At seventy-seven, he believed he still had plenty of good years left as a farmer; that, at least, was how his South Carolina home community had looked at it. But Urban Renewal held all the power. City Government was reveling in self-congratulation over attracting the Federal dollars, and they had no interest in anything outside their singular vision. Hundreds of Bottom families would benefit enormously, but not one.

Mr. Jackson visited his relatives back in South Carolina while the bulldozers destroyed his property. Returning to town, he moved into the elderly high-rise several blocks away. In his characteristic style, he tried to accommodate, but his heart was no longer in it. In less than two years, he died, "well taken care of."

His funeral was nearly surreal. The presiding pastor did a fine job, conducting an animated but respectful service. We sang, prayed, read Bible, and heard good words about the deceased. It was apparent, however, that the pastor knew Mr. Jackson only slightly. I empathized with him, because I had been in his position. For those of us who did know Mr. Jackson, a silent reality dominated his funeral: the giant of a man he had been and all he had accomplished. Anything else seemed trivial. Finally, toward the end of the service, Jimmie Pettigrew, who had no inclination to make public speeches but who could keep quiet no longer, asked if he could speak. "Mr. Jackson was one of the finest people ever to live in Eleventh Street Bottom. Most folks don't know that, but I was one of his neighbors from the day I was born. I want to thank Mr. Jackson for all he did for everyone. No matter what happens to

The Bottom, I will never forget this man." Jimmie sat down. There was a murmur of affirmation, but I knew there was great applause and cheering coming from many hearts.

Winston-Salem will never place an historical marker at the end of Dunleith Street to recognize the life and accomplishments of Hezekiah Jackson. I, however, would like to install one with the following inscription.

> On this land lived Hezekiah M Jackson, hero of the American promise. A native of a South Carolina farm, he moved here to work as a line laborer for R. J. Reynolds Tobacco Company. He lived frugally and saved, as his mother had taught him. He purchased a house and two lots and resided here for forty-five years. Mr. Jackson was a talented farmer, growing vegetables and sharing them up and down the street with his neighbors. Few were not touched by his generosity. He was a beloved spirit, creating goodwill all across Eleventh Street Bottom, one of the most deprived and downtrodden neighborhoods of the city. His work and life were ended by a very fine government program designed to benefit him. The program failed to take Mr. Jackson's uniqueness into account. Urban Renewal renewed his property but killed his spirit. So it is with vast human ventures: great communal virtue can mask severe individual damage. Helping the many can destroy the few. All of us need to remember that. Otherwise, our pride and self-proclamation will know no remorse, and we will take no interest in seeking better solutions.

Totally by chance, I recently had dinner with a man who had headed a major Winston-Salem foundation during that Urban Renewal era. Laughing heartily, he told me of a conversation between him and the director of the city's anti-poverty agency at that time. "The director told me that with the large number of bleeding-heart sentimentalists in our town, he fully expected someone to demand that several of those old slum houses in Eleventh Street Bottom be preserved as a museum. 'Even though we got those people something new and good,' he said, 'someone was bound to demand to hang onto what was old and bad.' We carried on that joke for several weeks," my dinner companion said, quite amused. I, myself, having known Mr. Jackson, found it harder to laugh.

12

The Mayfield Mandate

IN 1977 I became associate pastor of Highland Presbyterian Church. I was forty, still young compared to the membership of that ninety-six-year-old congregation, and no small bit intimidated.

One of my first acts was to form the Issues Class in the Sunday school, folks who would examine things going on in the larger community and talk with some of the people involved. Richard Nixon had recently connected the United States with China, a sleeping giant just beginning to wake up. "Understanding China Today" seemed a perfect Issues Class subject. I contacted the University of Louisville and found a young professor, Andrea McElderry, who was a China specialist and willing to speak. Dr. McElderry addressed perhaps forty people on the appointed Sunday morning, sketching China's history and stating what she thought were the essentials at present.

I thought she did a marvelous job. Not everyone present agreed, however. Retired Judge Ogden Peacock sprang to his feet challenging her view of post–World War II China and charging that China was a communist puppet of the Soviet Union. The judge gave Dr. McElderry a thorough scalding for being too naïve to see his point. I later learned that Ogden Peacock was an anchor member in the local John Birch Society.

As the Judge sat down, my nerves were shaking. What had I unleashed? Was the whole class going to agree with this man? Was the Issues Class a bad idea? I was most concerned with what Dr. McElderry would do next. It was then that a man, perhaps sixty, rose to his feet. "Who is he?" I asked myself, braced for what might come next. He was Mayfield Monroe, a well-liked, highly respected bachelor who had belonged to Highland Church for many years. He worked in the hardware business. Mayfield said, plainly and simply, "Judge Peacock, I spent several years in the army in China during and after World War II, and this young woman's presentation seems entirely accurate to what I experienced. I think she has done us a very fine job." Mayfield's words set the tone for the ensuing class discussion, and Judge Peacock was isolated. Dr. McElderry did not have to respond to him.

From that moment forward, Mayfield Monroe was *my friend*. I never forgot. Whenever I saw him, we had this special memory: the beautiful gift he had given exactly when I needed it most!

Seventeen years later, I, now the church's pastor, got a phone call from Mayfield Monroe. "Jim, will you perform my marriage?" In disbelief, I inquired. She was Elaine, an Episcopalian lady, a grandmother whose husband had died six years before. I had met Elaine several times but had no idea that confirmed bachelor Mayfield would actually take the step.

The marriage ceremony was wonderful: at home, with a house full of very happy people including Elaine's two daughters with families. In the years that followed, I visited Mayfield and Elaine regularly, and usually found the daughters there. Our visits seemed filled with hilarity and pleasure.

In 1998, Mayfield's doctors declared that he needed heart bypass surgery, that without it he would die soon. Mayfield would have none of it. "I refuse to spend several months in medical recovery," he said. "I've lived a good life, and whenever my time comes I want to die, not in a hospital." This sent alarm waves through the family. They loved the man, and they did not want to lose him prematurely! "We have to talk Mayfield into it!" I was told. I was asked to come join the persuasion team. I went, but after hearing the story fully, I took the position of supporting Mayfield in whatever decision he made. We wrangled, very forthrightly but also very fondly, and Mayfield finally won his case. They would not try to overrule him.

In September, 2001, I published a message in the church's newsletter announcing that I intended to retire in one year. I told the church that I would remain in the city as their friend, but that I no longer would serve in any way as their pastor. In other words, I would not participate in weddings or funerals. As soon as the letter came out, I got an urgent distress call from Elaine Monroe. "Jim! You have to promise me that there will be one exception to your policy! When Mayfield dies, you *have* to do the service. No one else can substitute. It has to be you. You've been too dear a friend. Promise me!"

A devilish thought entered my mind. "Elaine, how well do I know you? Well enough to say what I'm thinking? This could either seal or destroy our relationship."

Finally, I said it. "Elaine, you'll just have to tell Mayfield to die before September 1."

There was a stunned silence. Then an uproar of laughter! "Jim, who else would ever say that? I love you!" I had won. We held our two positions, but ended as before, cherished friends.

I saw them several times in my final year at Highland Church, often in worship, sometimes in their home.

Mayfield Monroe died of heart failure on August 22, 2002, eight days before I retired. His funeral was my final public act at Highland Church. Some things we do better not to try to figure out.

13

Clem's Visit

CLEMENT SPEAR had started his life on the cradle roll of the Highland Presbyterian Church. His attachment to this congregation was part of his life's definition. No one alive could remember a time when Clem had not been there. He was liked and respected.

There had been one moment in Clem's life, however, which he had deeply come to regret. He had owned a business downtown. On an impulse, he had filed a false tax return, trying to hide from view a number of thousands of dollars in business earnings. The Internal Revenue Service had been more savvy than he had thought. They had uncovered his misdeed, convicted him of tax fraud, and sent him to prison. His church, despite his wrong, had loved and supported him throughout. They knew he was a good man, and a single transgression had not changed that. They had written letters, visited him regularly, kept him in touch with events, helped his wife and family. When his prison term was finished, the church had welcomed him back like a returned brother. They harbored no malice, receiving him joyfully. He loved these people, and they loved him. Such was the life of Clement Spear, a man advanced in years by the time I became the church's pastor.

It happened one weekend that Jeremy Worth, an associate pastor, was preaching the Sunday sermon. Jeremy's standard practice was to use the empty sanctuary on Saturday afternoon to practice. Thus had he arrived at the church about 2:00 p.m. Jeremy had used his key to get in the fellowship hall door, and then, re-locking the door, had disarmed the burglar alarm. Passing through the empty church, Jeremy had entered the sanctuary, flipped on the lights and the sound system, and ascended the pulpit. He had practiced for maybe an hour.

Jeremy had then come down from the pulpit, turned off the sound system and lights, walked back through the empty building, and prepared to reset the burglar alarm before he left. The alarm would not reset, however. The control panel showed that there was an open connection in circuit five. Circuit five included the three large doors that led directly into the back of the sanctuary from outside the building.

Jeremy was perplexed. The burglar alarm had been set and the system fully closed when he had entered the building an hour before, meaning that the sanctuary doors had been shut. No one had entered or left the sanctuary during that hour; he had been there throughout. It was impossible that one of those doors could now be open.

Jeremy returned to the sanctuary and checked the outside doors. Sure enough, one was ajar. Why hadn't the alarm system picked this up earlier? He couldn't answer that and began to won-der what was going on. He shut the door securely and locked it, making sure its alarm contacts connected.

As he made his way back down the sanctuary aisle from the rear, he suddenly saw something he had not noticed before. A single hymnbook had been removed from its rack and was sitting on a pew seat. This was the only item out of place in the entire room; the sanctuary was otherwise perfectly prepared for worship the next morning. Jeremy looked at the book for a moment, won-dering how this had happened. Then it occurred to him. Clement Spear had died earlier that week. His funeral had been held the day before, on Friday afternoon. This hymnbook was in the seat

Clem had occupied for six decades. While he had been in prison, the church had "saved" the seat for him, telling him it was waiting, making it part of his welcome home.

The only explanation Jeremy could imagine was that, after his funeral, sometime during the night, Clem had decided to visit his beloved church one more time. He had entered by his normal route, sat in his seat, sung one or two favorite hymns, and departed. Who knows what sort of congregation had been present to sing with him? No other explanation ever emerged, even after a careful examination by the burglar alarm company. Apparently there are certain kinds of activity in this world that technology can not detect. The result of intense human relationship is one of them.

14

Mortified!

I HAD been a pastor at Highland Church for less than a month when an eighty-three-year-old woman, Alice Hill, passed away. Alice and her husband, Robert, had been church members for many years and knew my pastor colleague, Henry, very well. Henry, however, was away on a vacation trip. Because Alice had been sick before he left, Henry had told Robert that he would return immediately if Alice died. Robert had vetoed that idea, insisting that Henry go away, play golf, have a good time, and not worry. If anything happened, Robert said, he would figure out the best thing to do.

Alice had died three days into Henry's vacation. Henry immediately announced that he was coming home. "No, no," Robert had mandated. "You stay there! Reverend Chatham is here now, he's experienced, and he will do perfectly well with Alice's funeral. Everything will be fine."

Thus had Henry called to tell me the situation and to ask me to lead the funeral. He had also filled me in on the kind of person Alice was.

I called Robert immediately and went to visit. He gave me his own portrait of Alice. Robert was not what I would call a warm, gracious man, but I attributed this partly to his recent loss. He was friendly enough, and we got along well.

The funeral took place in a funeral home. Based upon Robert's description, I presented a brief portrait of Alice, offering thanksgiving for her life and for their life together. I praised God for claiming and possessing us from everlasting to everlasting. When it was finished, the friends and family expressed appreciation.

We were to bury Alice in the Lexington Cemetery, seventy-five miles east of our city. The funeral director asked if I wanted to ride in his car, and I accepted. I was placed in the back seat with Robert. For the entire seventy-five miles, Robert seemed strained and distant, barely engaging in conversation of any kind. I attributed this to his mourning, knowing that losing your wife of fifty-nine years is a mortal blow. After ninety minutes, we arrived at the cemetery and carried out the final ceremonies. Robert remained distant after the service and all the way back to Louisville. I was mystified.

As was my practice, I called him about two days later to visit. He accepted, again, however, in a distant tone. I had not been in his house two minutes before I got the full story.

"Reverend Chatham, my wife was a very private woman. There were things she did not want the world to know about her. One thing was her age. She was four years older than I, and she kept that a closely guarded secret all our married life. Never did *anyone* have the slightest hint. All it took was her funeral for the world to find out. You mentioned her birth date. Now, everyone knows! Mortified, she would have been mortified! You can not imagine how wrong it was for you to do that. It changed my whole attitude toward you and the church, and I haven't gotten over it one bit. The pain of losing my wife is bad enough, and now you add double pain on top of it."

I sat there shocked and mystified, wondering for a moment what flaw in me had created this travesty. I had, indeed, mentioned his wife's year of birth somewhere in my comments, reading it off the funeral information card, but the mention was at most fleeting.

I couldn't imagine that anyone had paid any attention, and, far more, that anyone cared. But none of this would soothe Mr. Hill.

"Reverend Chatham, in my will I have left fifty thousand dollars to Highland Presbyterian Church because I believed the church could be counted on to do well by me. Now I've changed my mind. I'm taking away that fifty thousand and leaving nothing. I can not give a penny to a place that has treated me so shabbily."

I apologized sincerely to Mr. Hill. I told him that hurting him was not at all my intention and that I deeply regretted having done it. I told him I knew nothing of his wife's wish and that I had meant nothing by my reference to her birth year. I told him I was profoundly sorry, all to no avail. He was bitter, and he had no intention of becoming less so. I departed on that note. A few days later, I called again, but he refused to see me this time.

When Henry returned from vacation, Robert Hill told him the entire story. Henry met with me the next day. "Well, Rob Hill called last night, and it sounds like things didn't go too well."

"Not very well, Henry. I knew nothing about Mrs. Hill's super-sensitivity."

"It's the most ridiculous thing I've ever heard of," Henry said. "Imagine, how she kept that stuff pent up inside all her life. Why would anyone care? I've known them for years and have never thought about her age one way or the other. Neither has anyone else."

"I'm also sorry about the fifty thousand dollars," I said. "Here I am, having just arrived at Highland, and I've already cost us a bundle of money."

"Chatham, don't worry about that. We didn't want the fifty thousand. It was slumlord money, made off of renting miserable old houses to poor people in the West End. That was how Rob got it, rent money on shacks not fit to live in. We're better off without that money."

In the years I worked with Henry, I never respected him more than in that moment.

15

Angels and Satellites

EDDIE HACK was a small, wiry man, an ex-baseball shortstop. Married to Gladys, Eddie, in his late seventies, was still spirited and alert, with plenty of the infielder's pepper in his personality. Gladys was a member of Highland Presbyterian Church. Eddie was Roman Catholic.

I learned that Eddie was in St. Anthony's Hospital for a medical procedure. I went to visit.

Our conversation was typical. Eddie read every word written on the sports pages, and he had a commentary on all of it. "The hardest, meanest fastball I ever saw was from Bob Gibson. That guy could flat bring it! And he wouldn't hesitate to take your chin off if you got too close to the plate. He struck the fear of God into everybody. Always made you know who was boss. Like you were a guest standing at his home plate, and he'd give you a chance only if you were respectful. Did you know that that dude once pitched with a broken leg?

"Joe Namath may have been the best passing quarterback in history, but he sure couldn't move. If not for a solid offensive line, he was dead meat. Easiest target a charging linebacker could ever ask for. You could telegraph that you were coming, and he'd still be there when you arrived.

"I saw Hogan and Arnold Palmer and Nicklaus all play, and I can tell you that Hogan was the best of the lot. A little steel man! He didn't have the power of the others, but he could thread the needle with his shots. If he wanted it to sail between two tree limbs and land left-front on the green, then it would sail right between the two limbs and end up left-front. That man was a wizard with a golf club.

"The most memorable play of my career happened one night down in Birmingham. We were playing Savannah, and they had runners on first and second with no outs. This strong, powerful kid named Roger Beasley came to the plate, and on the first pitch he hit a shot to the left of the pitcher's mound. I knew he tended to hit up the middle, so I was shaded a step toward second. When the ball hit his bat, I broke by instinct. It was the right instinct. The ball rocketed straight into my path two steps from second. I caught it waist high, stepped on second and saw the runner coming at me from first base. He was frantically trying to reverse direction. I ran right at him and tagged him out. Unassisted triple play: it felt *soooo* sweet! I can still remember the sensation!"

All I had to do was nudge Eddie's memory, and out would pour a couple more sports tales.

After twenty minutes, Eddie's hospital room door opened. In walked about the most bedraggled, deadpan nun I had ever seen, a woman who appeared to have been at this duty far too long, thoroughly bored. She embodied the opposite of Eddie's vigor, and I almost wondered if the wrong person was the patient. The nun carried a clipboard. With no expression of personality and no greeting, she looked down at the clipboard. "Ahhhh, Mr. Pack. No, Mr. Hack. That's your name, Hack."

"That's right, sister, I'm Eddie Hack."

"Mr. Hack, Father is coming down the hall with the holy sacrament." Her words sounded like they were coming from a robot. She was looking at the clipboard, not at Eddie. "Will you want to receive it this morning?"

Eddie, engrossed in telling a baseball tale, replied, "No thank you, Sister, I think I'll pass today."

Never looking up from the clipboard, and still without even a glimmer of facial expression, the nun droned, "You mean you don't want to be with the holy angels up in heaven?"

"Do I believe what I just heard?" I asked myself. "Is it deadpan jest? Or does she expect Eddie to believe it? Does the priest coming down the hall believe it? How can Eddie respond?"

Eddie never hesitated. "Sister, with all those satellites flying around up there, I don't think I want to be around. It's gotten too dangerous."

Without looking up from the clipboard, the nun said with an air of resignation, "Okay." I was about to burst, trying not to laugh. The nun made a mark on her clipboard, turned, and left the room.

At his funeral a couple of years later, I was visualizing the holy angels up in heaven clearing space amid all those satellites, making a place for Eddie.

16

The Ultimate Why?

HUMAN LIFE should not let this happen. Jessie Hobbs was ten years old, a big kid with a black burr cut. His mother, Kathleen Hobbs, had grown up in Highland Presbyterian Church, but later had moved to a very popular independent church near where she lived. Grandmother, Dorothea Gibson, remained at Highland, a devoted member over many decades. I had not known daughter or grandson before, but grandmother Dorothea I counted as a dear friend. She radiated warmth and grace.

Young Jessie Hobbs was diagnosed with leukemia. It was unbelievable: strong, healthy, good-looking Jessie, dying. Medical science could nibble around the edges of this dreaded blood cancer, perhaps slowing it down, but the disease would win. The end for Jessie would probably come sooner instead of later.

When I heard it, I made an appointment to visit Dorothea. She invited her daughter, Kathleen, and grandson, Jessie. I had not expected that but welcomed it. After the four of us conversed a bit (entering the world of a ten-year-old is not my forte), Jessie went off to pursue an interest in some other part of the house. Kathleen and Dorothea filled me in on details. They were hiding nothing from Jessie, but neither did they want this to dominate his life, even though it was clearly dominating theirs.

We mourned together, asked the eternally unanswerable question, "Why?" and prayed for healing if that were possible, strength if it was not. We read several Bible passages, and renewed our confidence in the love and care of the One in whom we all believed. It was a good moment, even in a terrible time.

The cancer showed no mercy. A few months later, Jesse died. An essential piece of everyone in the family was ripped away. The emptiness descended and dwelt heavily.

I went to Jessie's funeral primarily to support my friend and church member Dorothea, and also Kathleen. The funeral was under the leadership of Kathleen's pastor, a man of considerable oratorical talents. A throng attended in a funeral home chapel.

"I want to assure you," the pastor began, "that we do not have to worry about this young man. His faith in God was rock solid! Through months of illness, not once did he complain. Never was he threatened by doubt. He trusted God to sustain him through everything. Not a word of anger. Not a moment of questioning. Young Jessie Hobbs was exemplary, setting a marvelous example for the rest of us."

I thought to myself, "That's a strange way to describe an eleven-year-old. I've never known one like that, but maybe so. I only knew Jesse from brief moments. Maybe his pastor knew more."

"And Jessie's mother Kathleen, has been strong, too," the pastor continued. "Never once complaining. Never questioning God's love. Like Abraham, she trusted her only son to God's all-powerful hands, knowing that he had been a gift and rejoicing in the time she had with him. She didn't ask, 'Why my Jessie?' That could easily have dominated her outlook, but no. She knew that her present grief amounts to nothing compared to the glory to be revealed. Kathleen's faith is an example for all of us to follow, strong, unwavering."

I knew Kathleen a bit by now, and, despite her virtues which were many, these words didn't fit her either. I wondered if the pastor wasn't telling us more about his own needs than about Kathleen.

He continued. "Perhaps some of you remember the story that appeared in Life Magazine after World War II. A fighter pilot, one of the heroes of the war, had been away from home for three years. When the war ended, he flew his plane back into the airport in his hometown. He circled the field once and brought the plane in on the main runway. Pulling off onto the grass, he parked and climbed out. He headed toward the airport terminal. It was then that he saw running toward him his family. The Life Magazine photographer was in the perfect position to take a picture from behind the pilot, over his left shoulder. The photo showed the pilot striding forward with his family running at him across the tarmac. One of his children held aloft a sign with huge words, *welcome home!*

"This is why God has called Jessie to heaven," the pastor said, "so that when we arrive, someone we love will come running toward us carrying that same huge sign, *welcome home!* Jesse has gone ahead to prepare our way."

The pastor prayed a brief prayer and then exited by the center aisle of the funeral chapel.

I slowly followed the crowd out the back door. The large driveway outside was covered with people standing and talking. Most of them I did not know. I scanned for a familiar face. I spotted one, a woman I much liked and respected, the mother of one of my son's high school classmates. This woman saw me and waved a hand in recognition. Working my way through the gathering, I came toward her. She had a strained, agitated look. "By golly, am I glad to see you," she greeted me. "I need a preacher right now. You are going to tell me every good reason you know of why an eleven-year-old should have to die of cancer, and while you're telling me, you need to understand that I'm not going to believe a single damned word you say!"

I looked at her. "I think you and I have just had the same experience. Every honest feeling inside me has just been suppressed and denied."

"Exactly!" she said. "I have been told that I am not supposed to raise critical questions before God, that I should bury all my upset and pain, be quiet and pretend that faith makes everything in my life fine. Well, I'm not made that way! A wonderful young life has just been taken away for no good reason, and I'm mad as hell. And don't try to tell me I shouldn't be!"

We embraced in the greeting of friends.

17

Gonzo Funeralism

BETWEEN THE two large stone columns at the front entrance of Cave Hill Cemetery moved a jet-black limo with heavily darkened windows. It advanced up the long entrance driveway past the line of waiting cars. It stopped at the far end in full view of everyone gathered. We were ten minutes past the scheduled time for the funeral. We had been waiting for this arrival, not having any idea what to expect or whether to expect anything. Both the timing and the limo-look were carefully designed to make a statement: "I want privacy, but I want to be seen by everyone. I want the dark-on-black of this vehicle to shroud me in intrigue, but I don't want any of the people gathered for little brother's funeral to miss my arrival!" The message was plain.

As the limo stood in the middle of the long driveway in view of everyone, the left-side-rear door opened, and out stepped a tall-ish, slender male wearing jeans, a tee shirt, and sun glasses. He placed the sun glasses on top of the limo, peeled off the tee shirt, and tossed it back inside. Out a window, someone handed him a towel. He wiped his head and upper body. He handed the towel back inside and was given a red-and-brown plaid shirt. He put it on. Then a jacket. Leaning down, he gazed into the blackened limo window at his reflection. Ready at last, with the entire procession having watched his personal preparations—whether we wanted to or not—he climbed back into the limo. It pulled into its place in the funeral line, and we moved slowly toward the grave.

A long-inactive member of Highland Presbyterian Church, James Thompson, had died. I had not known Jimmy Thompson, but I had enjoyed periodic visits with his mother, Virginia Thompson. Mrs. Thompson was a spirited, friendly woman who had fascinating stories about raising her three boys. "Davison was a nice young man, a straight edge, headed directly toward wherever he was going," she had said. "He had success written all over him from the beginning. Hunter was a nice boy too, but he was always following his own route, not the path anyone else had laid out. And Jimmy was the youngest, trying to keep up with his brothers. I loved every minute of it, raising those boys," she had said. "I miss it now. Life is a lot more routine. But they stay in touch."

Third son, Jimmy, had died. Today was the day of his funeral.

Family and friends had gathered. There must have been thirty cars lined up on the long, stately, tree-lined driveway of Cave Hill Cemetery. Our plan was to convene everyone in the driveway and proceed to the grave for the funeral service. The event had gone well so far, except that no one knew where Hunter was, or whether he was coming. Word of Jimmy's death had been left for him, but he had not replied. Surely he would come? When the black limo materialized, there was a collective sigh of relief. Hunter was barely late. And even if he had made his final preparations in the cemetery driveway, creating a spectacle not previously witnessed along the hallowed lanes of Louisville's most venerable burial ground, everyone knew that thumbing his nose at venerability was part of Hunter's style, and that nothing should be taken seriously. What would have really disappointed Mama would have been if he hadn't come at all. We were okay.

Hunter S. Thompson, nationally known writer and journalist, founder of what he himself labeled "gonzo journalism," had grown up as a member of Highland Presbyterian Church. A talented if unorthodox teenager, he had become part of the "New

Journalism" movement of the 1960s and had created his own style. His writings set forth in direct, usually crude, always colorful, highly imaginative, passionately offensive language his cynical opinions on politics, American life, the South, and anything else he took a mind to describe. He frequently included reference to his own drug and alcohol use. *Fear and Loathing in Las Vegas*, possibly his best-known book, told of his drug-laden trip to cover for *Rolling Stone* magazine a district attorney's anti-drug conference in Vegas. *The Rum Diaries* was his only novel. *The Proud Highway: the Saga of a Desperate Southern Gentleman*, was a collection of his letters. In *Hell's Angels* he chronicled his year with the notorious motorcycle gang. *Generation of Swine* was his lament on American youth of the 1980s. And *Better Than Sex* was his account of Bill Clinton's 1992 Presidential victory.

He wrote for several journals, most notably *Rolling Stone*. In 1970, he ran for sheriff of Pitkin County, Colorado, on the Freak Power Party ticket, whose main platform was to decriminalize drugs. He narrowly lost. He was, we were told, the model for Gary Trudeau's character, Duke, in the *Doonesbury* comic strip.

My impression of Hunter S. Thompson was that he was brilliant, confrontingly forthright, off-the-wall, rich, outrageous, purposely offensive, lacking any shred of social grace in his writings, the ultimate I-don't-give-a-damn-about-anything-or-anybody-but-myself personality. He lived in a world that required no accountability, and he granted none. He was disgusting and intriguing at the same time. I wondered if he had a mellow and compassionate side. If he did, he specialized in hiding it. We who live relatively ordered and disciplined lives enjoy a peek once in a while into the totally bizarre, and Hunter Thompson provided it.

At the grave site, we gathered under a cemetery tent. I called the funeral service to order, prayed for God's presence, offered an interpretation of life and death taken from the Psalms and from the writings of St. Paul, spoke of James Thompson's life, and ended with a benediction. Most of the people present I did not know. Several introduced themselves and spoke their appreciation. Jimmy's mother offered particular thanks. At length, the tallish man stood in front of me, offered his hand, and said, "I'm Hunter Thompson, and I want to thank you for the service." He also mentioned the name of the young woman at his side. I greeted them both. Having read Hell's Angels plus several of his magazine essays, I wondered if I had just witnessed one of the few polite moments in Hunter Thompson's public life. Was he being genuine, or had this moment been created by propriety's constraint? Was he roiling inside to escape this smothering cemetery and become his caustic, cynical self again? I would have also liked to have heard his commentary on the words I had just spoken, on the Christian theology of life and death. I would have probably found it angry and disgusting, but also possessing honest human insights, well worth my hearing. No doubt that Hunter Thompson was brilliant.

I wished that some family member or friend had invited all of us over for food and conversation after the funeral, as sometimes happens. What I most wanted to see was Hunter Thompson bantering with his mother, she, the one person in the world who knew him better than he knew himself. She had the personality to stand toe-to-toe with him and, in a mother's fondness, challenge the founder of Gonzo Journalism. I suspect it would have been electric. A missed opportunity; I was sorry.

I noted that as Hunter and his young female escort made their way across the cemetery grass back toward the limo, she seemed to be expending considerable attention on keeping him vertical. Probably all my wishes were useless. Who can guess what was circulating in his brain?

Several years later, mother, Virginia Thompson, died. She had by then moved out of her condominium into a high-end nursing home. I was called by Hunter's brother Davison to lead that funeral as well. Davison said that his mother wanted her service held at the nursing home. Her current friends lived there, and there was no need in making them travel elsewhere.

I arrived at the appointed day and time. Davison, looking entirely corporate in a gray business suit, greeted me and thanked me for coming. We walked to the nursing home chapel where the funeral service was to be held. Several people were already in place, and others were slowly arriving. Front-and-center in the room, dwarfing the speaker's podium which stood behind it, was a double-huge arrangement of flowers, a display of pink and white blossoms radiating outward in a sunburst. It would have fitted well into the Washington Cathedral; it was far too big for this space. A card hung from the flower vase. I worked my hand through the flowers and twisted open the card. "Rolling Stone." Perfect: totally out of bounds.

Davison said to me, "I've got a problem. Read this." He handed me a two-page, typed letter. It was from a friend of Hunter's. It began, "Hunter, baby, that mother of yours was *one hell-l-l of a woman!*" It went on to recount a party this friend had attended where he had met Virginia. They had talked and laughed and joked, and had a few drinks. He had found her to be "a killer," "a jiving-ass grandma," "full of hot stuff." And now he had sent this letter of praise filled with vivid expletives. The final line said, "Read this at her funeral so that the whole damned world will know what a hell of a woman she was."

I looked across the room at those gathered for the funeral: ninety and ninety-five year olds in wheelchairs, others on walkers, others tottering slowly, nurses, caregivers, all appearing to be possessed with common sense, propriety, and reasonably good manners. I could visualize Davison or me standing before this group and reading, "Hunter, baby, that mother of yours was *one hell-l-l of a woman!*"

"What do you think we ought to do?" Davison asked.

"I wouldn't touch it," I replied.

"But it's written to Hunter."

"Then give it to Hunter. It's not written for this gathering. They would be appalled," I said. "Either appalled or titillated," I realized in my mind. Let's not underestimate ninety-year-olds.

"That's what I think too. I was just trying to convince myself," said Davison.

"No letter?" I said.

"No letter," he affirmed. He stuffed it back in his coat pocket. I wish to this day I had stuffed it in mine.

People gathered for the funeral until the room was full: more wheelchairs, more walkers. We waited. Davison had received no word from Hunter but assumed he would appear. I was hoping it would not be in the same style as the last occasion. We waited longer. No Hunter. Finally, Davison signaled, "Let's go ahead. We can't keep these people waiting." Throughout the service, I tried to stop myself from noticing every movement at the back door, thinking that no man would decide to miss his mother's funeral. The service proceeded without incident; no Hunter.

Around a decade later, on February 20, 2005, Hunter S. Thompson ended his own life, shooting himself in the kitchen of his home in Aspen, Colorado. Friends, according to the national media, guessed it was because of his despondence over his declining health.

On Saturday, August 20, 2005, a memorial party was held at Thompson's home. There were readings by Lyle Lovett and performances by the Nitty Gritty Dirt Band and other rock groups. The guest list of two hundred fifty included Ralph Steadman, Thompson's longtime illustrator, and actors Sean Penn, Bill Murray, and Johnny Depp. Security guards kept the public away, but Hunter Thompson fans perched themselves in the surrounding hills for the best view they could find of the celebration.

The high moment came when Thompson's ashes, at his specification, were blasted into the sky from atop a fifteen-story tower modeled on Thompson's logo, a clinched fist, made symmetrical by two thumbs, rising from the hilt of a dagger. Accompanied by red, white, blue, and green fireworks, the deafening boom of the blast shook the ground and could be heard for miles around.

I was not invited. Oh, shucks!

18

Cassie's Torment

CASSIE WAS driving out Bardstown Road one afternoon with her nine-year-old daughter. Bardstown Road is a busy, though not terribly hurried, two-lane thoroughfare in southeast Louisville, and Cassie was moving with the traffic. In an instant, a woman dashed in front of her car. The woman had gotten off a bus on a side street and was trying to transfer. The "thud" was heavy and horrible. The woman died instantly.

Cassie was dazed, shocked, horrified. No warning, it just happened! Witnesses agreed that Cassie had not been speeding; it would have been nearly impossible in the traffic. No charges were filed. The police called Cassie's best friend, Marlene, for help. Marlene and husband Charlie came quickly, took Cassie and her daughter home, and cared for the car.

The days that followed were torment for Cassie. She kept re-living what had happened: fine afternoon, driving along, woman, loud thud, horror! Was there something she could have done to prevent it? Should she have seen the woman? It happened lightning fast; the woman was just *there*! The awful sound, and then the body flying forward to sprawl on the pavement, not moving! The images rolled through Cassie's head.

About the third day, she started making regular visits to me. On each visit she re-told the story. "I keep seeing it happen. When

I'm awake, when I'm asleep, when I'm doing the laundry, when I'm helping Sharon with her homework, when I'm eating: here comes that dreaded scene again. I've been taken over by a premonition: something else is about to happen! I can't go near the car. Don't know when I'll drive again. The idea of climbing into that driver's seat is too painful to face.

"I need to go see her family—for my own sake! Tell them how sorry I am. Tell them how I regret what happened. Cry with them. The funeral was two days ago, and I needed to be there. I was part of that woman's life. I needed to stand at her grave arm-in-arm with everyone saying goodbye. But my lawyer said, 'Absolutely no! No contact! You are to say nothing. We don't know what will happen, and until we do know, you aren't to speak a word!' That's about the harshest order I've ever received. My insides are aching to act human."

Cassie repeated essentially this same account six or eight times over a month. Her pain was not diminishing.

One Friday afternoon I had an idea. I said to Cassie, "Will you follow me for the next few minutes in an experience I think might be worthwhile? I'm not going to tell you what will happen; I just want you to do what I say. Is that okay?"

"Sure, Jim, at this point, I'm open to whatever you think might be good."

"Wait here. I'll be right back." I scoured the building, looking for people. I found a church member creating a bulletin board, a preschool teacher preparing her room, two members of the maintenance staff who were putting away dishes and glasses in the kitchen, a woman from the refugee ministry office, and one or two others. We assembled in the front of the empty worship sanctuary, seven of us in a cavernous room that held four hundred.

"I need your help," I told them. I briefly recounted what had happened to Cassie several weeks before. "We are going to hold a funeral right here right now. I'm going to bring Cassie in among us, and we will gather around her and create a memorial service for Millie Henderson. I want you to be Millie's family, her friends. I want you to be Cassie's family, her friends. I want you to stand by her, support her, speak to her, listen to her, love her. We will commit Millie Henderson into the hands of Almighty God, pray for her family, and console Cassie whose car killed her. Is everybody willing?" I was gazing intently into their eyes, trying to convey what was at stake.

Slight pause. "I'm in," said one.

"Thank you, dear soul," my mind answered.

"Me too," another.

"Let's do it. I don't have the slightest idea what I'm doing, but we'll do our best." The group glued together in mutual uncertainty and commitment.

I returned to my office, picked my liturgical service book off the shelf, and brought Cassie into the sanctuary. She knew everyone there. "We're going to have a funeral for Millie Henderson," I said. "We will give thanks for her life, what we know of it, and mourn her tragic death. We are all human beings, and we know the meaning of loss, no matter who it is."

I worked through a shortened funeral service. We read Scripture. We prayed. We shared our humanity and our faith. As we reached the end of the liturgy, we sang one halting but determined verse of "Blessed Be the Tie That Binds."

"Now, let us draw into a close circle and join arms." We did. "Stand in silence for a few moments and prepare to say whatever you feel led to say, whatever enters your mind. You don't have to say anything, but if you have something to say, this is your opportunity." We were quiet.

"All right, now speak, if you want."

Silence. From long ago I had learned to wait and trust.

"I've been feeling very deeply for Ms. Henderson's family," one person finally said. "Our family lost one of our members not long ago, and it's hard. There's a big hole left that nothing fills. No one takes the place of Aunt Mable. And I've also been feeling for

Cassie. God, what must it be like to have been driving that car? How could you ever get over it, even though it wasn't your fault. I can feel what must have been going on in her these weeks, and I hope that from somewhere she can find the strength to move beyond it."

Others followed with similar comments. "Cassie, here is what happened in my life. I feel your pain!"

Finally, Cassie spoke. She poured forth: "I killed a woman. It could have been a member of *my* family. That's with me day and night. I pray that God will forgive me. I didn't mean to do it, God knows that, but I still need forgiveness." I was glad Cassie's lawyer was not present. "And I pray that the family can forgive me. It's their horrible loss. No one will take the place of their mother and sister. I only wish I could tell them how sorry I am. I hope they can hear me right now across the distance. I hope my voice will somehow reach them. Can that be possible?"

Cassie broke down in tears. The group spontaneously circled her, enclosed her, hugged her, joined quietly in her tears, embraced her one-by-one, and then formed a circle around her.

"Into God's almighty and loving hands do we commit Millie Henderson," I concluded, "and may the power of God's Spirit sustain Cassie from this day forward."

After a communal hug, it was over. We left the sanctuary with an intense feeling of camaraderie, even as we went our separate ways.

Cassie's visits became less frequent. Soon she was coming mostly to catch me up on legal happenings. She also went back to driving. Several times, she spoke her appreciation.

A year later she reported to me, "It's settled. No charges, no lawsuit. We're clear. The family called me to talk. They said that right after the accident, they wanted more than anything else to contact me, to assure me that they knew I wasn't to blame, that they didn't hold anything against me. But their lawyer told them,

"Absolutely no! No contact! We don't know what will happen here, and until we find out, you are not to say a word!"

Here had been two badly hurting families, both wanting to reach out and heal each other, but both forbidden by their lawyers. Something was drastically wrong in this picture.

19

Encounter with the Unknown

I HAVE known a few rare people in my lifetime who have actually loved associating with thirteen-year-olds. Amanda Craft was one of them. Five days a week, Amanda taught middle school in the public system. On Sunday mornings she taught middle school Sunday school, and on Sunday nights she was a junior high youth group adviser at Highland Church. She found vigor and excitement in the new discoveries her young adolescents were making about life, in their mood swings, and in their sometimes bizarre behavior. Amanda was a wonderful, hearty, dependable person.

Thus was it absolutely crushing when Amanda learned that she had AIDS. She had contracted pneumonia, it had gotten much worse, and she had been hospitalized, leading to the diagnosis. It was total shock. No one had any idea how her infection had happened.

We were in the 1980s, on the front edge of the AIDS phenomenon. A few articles had appeared in national news media warning of this deadly menace, but it still seemed mostly far away on another continent. Then suddenly, it was in our midst, happening to one of our cherished own. Amanda was given the best treatment the medical community knew how to give. She was said to be in an advanced stage.

Visiting her in the hospital was a production. Before entering her room, I had to wash my hands and arms with disinfectant soap, put on a complete covering over my body and limbs, wear gloves and shoe covers, and fit over my head a hood that filtered my breathing and talking. My only unimpeded contact was by vision through a small slit in the hood. I was to stand across the room from Amanda, not getting close and certainly not touching her or anything else other than the door knob. I wondered how Amanda felt about being visited by a space creature. I had to tell her who I was. I went through this procedure five or six times.

Common wisdom at that time believed that AIDS was probably transmitted through body fluids, and that casual relatedness probably held little risk. But no one was certain. Could the virus travel through simple touch, or through air? There had not been enough study to know. Amanda was this hospital's second AIDS patient, and the medical staff was in no mood to take risks.

How should Amanda's situation be interpreted to the church? The pastoral staff had to answer this question fast. I made it a practice not to be a conduit for medical information among members, and Amanda would be no exception. She, however, had worked for several years at the heart of our youth program, and we couldn't let the news seep out slowly, as if we wanted to hide it.

We decided that our message needed to be the hospital's message: that we did not think there was any danger, but that no one could be sure. Even that word, we knew, would land heavily on the parents of affected teenagers. We had learned from experience that rational human beings can assume entirely new personalities when protecting their own young.

We decided to assemble immediately the junior high parents and hope we could have a good discussion. Mercifully, it worked. They shared our leeriness, but no one launched into paranoia. With the junior high parents setting the mood, the larger church followed. Thank God! We avoided a frenzy of angst.

The next question was: what happens when Amanda dies? The hospital settled that fast: we cremate her! Her remains were to be buried in a family plot near her childhood home in Virginia, and the medical staff insisted that the uncertainties of transport and burial required cremation. They even wanted the canister that held her tightly sealed. Such was the AIDS scare: uncertainty pervaded everything.

Amanda's funeral was huge: students from the public school where she had taught, youth and parents from our church, and a large contingent of her social and artistic friends from across the city. She had been a winsome human being, and the multitude wanted to speak their farewell. Her father, who must have been his daughter's role model for pleasantness, expressed the family's gratitude.

Throughout the funeral, however, a larger consciousness was present. Yes, we had lost Amanda, which was terrible, but also we were now in a new era. *AIDS was present among us*, no longer just an ominous cloud on the distant horizon, and there was no trusted prescription on relating to it. We needed to become wary and cautious, but exactly how to do that was uncertain. We would be facing a dangerous enemy whose war tactics were unknown. That could turn us into different people, and we might well not like the result.

20

Larry's Legacy

LARRY, OUR next-door neighbor, died of AIDS. He was a professor at the medical school, sociable, vibrant. Larry lived in the lower half of a duplex rented from its owner, Mrs. Street. Outside his teaching, Larry had one devotion: turning Mrs. Street's property into an arboretum. He was an avid horticulturalist, planting exotic perennials, nurturing them, watering them, weeding them, and loving them so that they responded with royal beauty. Neighbors would walk in from blocks around to sample the wonders of Larry's work. The two of us would arrive home from somewhere, walk up onto our front porch, and be greeted by an excited Larry, "Jim, Nancy, let me show you what I found at the garden center *today*!" Another horticultural lovely fit for a queen's palace.

Larry was HIV-positive for a lengthy period, but then contracted AIDS. Nancy and I could see that his normal complexion was turning pale and sallow, that he was gaunt and frail. But his illness bore one reverse effect. The sicker he became, the more intense he became toward his garden. It had been an addiction before; now it became an obsession. Larry tended every square foot of the property, related to every plant, is if it were a piece of his soul. He seemed to be trying to extend his own life through his plants, to keep himself alive by making them healthy and vigorous. If *he* didn't have a future, at least *they* would.

His death was sad and heavy across the neighborhood. Larry had lived there for a more than a decade, and he was integral to the friendship network. We mourned.

Funeral arrangements were to be handled by his extended family a long distance away, but we neighbors wanted to honor him as well. He did not have any faith connections we knew of. We did not want to do anything out of character for him, such as imposing a religious facade on his death.

We finally realized what to do. One Saturday afternoon, Larry's favorite gardening time, we set up a circle of folding chairs in his backyard. More than a dozen neighbors joined the circle. Various people spoke of their relationships with Larry, how they would remember him: friendly, animated, intelligent, knowledgeable, in love with his garden and plants. Someone read a poem about human oneness with the natural world. Then we walked together through his yard, examining his gorgeous products.

One thing bore into our minds. We knew that Mrs. Street, the property owner, had no interest in Larry's horticulture. When she hired a lawn company to cut the grass, her order was simple and straightforward: *a crew cut!* Whatever grew was to be lowered to ground level. Larry had managed to keep her instincts at bay during his time there, but Mrs. Street had a short memory. We could all envision the mass murder that would happen a few days later and the dust cloud that would be set adrift through the neighborhood.

And then someone had a brilliant idea. "Let's each of us go home and get a shovel and transplant two or three plantings into our own yard and nurture them forward. We'll each carry forward a piece of Larry. He will smile!"

" Is it illegal? Will we be stealing what now belongs to Mrs. Street?"

"Probably, but are you kidding? In a day or two, Mrs. Street's yard maniacs will saw down everything here. She'll never know the difference. We need to act while we can."

"What better way to honor Larry than to do with his plants what he would do?"

"I'll feel like an imposter, but let's try it," someone said.

Everyone left and returned with shovels and carts. Someone dug up the gloxinia, someone else the phalaenopsis, someone else the bromeliad, and the kalanchoe. Plants big and small landed in nearby gardens. People worked, laughed, helped one another, expressed their regrets, and quietly rejoiced. Larry's death was terrible, but his legacy lived.

21

Losing Her Faith?

"JIM, PLEASE come fast. I'm afraid Paula is losing her faith!"

Paula was a rare human being, highly intelligent, incomparably kind, and endlessly self-giving. Her own children sometimes called her "Saint Paula." She was the director of a speech and hearing center for children, speech therapy being her specialty. I never saw her at work, but if it was anything like her presence in the wider world, then it was remarkable.

Tragically, Paula had been diagnosed with breast cancer, aggressive. Her medical team had tried everything they knew: surgery, radiation, drug treatments. Her friends prayed for her in volumes, and good wishes poured in. But nothing slowed the progress. Paula had remained hopeful and confident for months, but then the inevitable had become apparent. She began to look anemic and downcast, as if she were a hundred years old rather than sixty. It was painful to watch.

I visited her many times, mostly at home. As her pastor I did not hesitate to inquire directly into her heart and soul. "What are you experiencing, Paula? Thinking? Feeling? Are there good times, and can you tell me what they are? What happens in the worst times?" We would look each other straight in the eye and have authentic conversations.

Her companion, Fran, called on this particular afternoon. "Jim, please come fast. I'm afraid Paula is losing her faith."

Fran had been Paula's closest female friend for years. Through parenthood and beyond, these two had depended on each other. Now that Paula was sick, Fran was hardly leaving her side, managing Paula's care. I went immediately. Fran met me outside Paula's front door.

"Jim, it's terrible! Paula is saying things I know she doesn't believe. She told me she is no longer even sure there is a God, that she certainly has not seen much evidence of it lately. She's wondering if faith is a sham, a grand illusion. Go inside and talk to her and see what you can do. Please!"

Paula was direct and honest. "I feel like shit, Jim. I hurt most of the time. I don't have enough energy to do half of what I want to do. I look awful. Instead of learning and growing, I'm shrinking and shriveling. Each day is worse than the one before. I hate it that people are having to do so much to keep me going. Did I do something wrong? Is God punishing me for something I don't know about? How can a God of love put me and everyone else through this misery?"

But then she also said other things. "I look out the window at the fall trees and am overwhelmed by the beauty I live in. I think of my three children, what joy they are. I have the most wonderful friends. How could I ask for more? My life has been filled with blessings.

"Sometimes I curse God, sometimes I praise God. I feel better, I feel worse. I laugh, I cry. Will you read to me the twenty-third psalm? That's the most comforting experience I have right now."

At Paula's funeral not long afterward, I said, "In these recent months, our cherished friend Paula has been through a jungle of emotions. 'Bless the Lord, O my soul, and all that is within me bless his holy name' (Ps 103:1); at times, these words have spoken for her. 'How long, O Lord? Will you hide yourself forever? How long will your wrath burn like fire?' (Ps 89:46); at times, these words have spoken for her. 'The Lord is good; his steadfast love endures forever, and his faithfulness to all generations' (Ps 100:5); at times, these words have spoken for her. 'My God, my God, why have you forsaken me? Why are you so far from helping me, from the words of my groaning?' (Ps 22:1); at times, these words have spoken for her. 'Even though I walk through the darkest valley, I fear no evil; for you are with me; your rod and your staff–they comfort me' (Ps 23:4); at times, these words have spoken for her. Whether in joy or in turmoil, in heartfelt thanksgiving or in anguished lament, Paula has belonged to God. Let us give thanks for God's faithfulness."

Where did we get the notion that, when we are relating to God, we need to be polite, covering over true feelings? Certainly not from the Bible.

22

Terror on the Interstate

"OH, MY God! I can't believe that idiot!" I said to myself as we turned right out of the funeral home parking lot onto Dutchman's Lane. I wanted to blow my horn, blink my headlights, do anything to get him to turn around and abide by the admonitions of sanity. But, no, it was too late. There were now four, six, eight cars in procession with many more to come, and turning them all around would have been nearly impossible. From here, we just had to take our chances.

I had led many services at this funeral home through the years. The place had frequently seemed quirky. One staff member, for instance, had only a single thing to say to me no matter the situation, "Pastor, wouldn't you like to have a little prayer with the family?" I would meet with the deceased's relatives to make funeral arrangements, and the first thing out of his mouth would be,"Pastor, wouldn't you like to have a little prayer with the family?" I would attend the visitation, and as I was leaving, he would intercept me and ask, "Pastor, wouldn't you like to stay around until it's over and then have a little prayer with the family?" My phone would ring, and he would be on the line, "The sons and daughters have come by to drop off photographs. While they're here, wouldn't you like to come over and have a little prayer with the family?"

On this day, perhaps a hundred people had attended the service at the funeral home, and it appeared that at least half of them would be traveling to the cemetery. There was a perfectly good route for getting there. Turn left out of the funeral home parking lot, travel half a block onto Dutchman's Lane, turn right into Taylorsville Road, travel a mile and a half, veer right onto Bardstown Road, and travel three miles to the main cemetery entrance on the right. There would be stop lights along the way and our procession would get chopped into pieces, but it was a simple route and we could wait for one another at the end. The route would be very easy and very safe. Why would I have thought to discuss it with the funeral director?

But, no, we turned right out of the parking lot, and I knew instantly what that meant. We were getting on I-64 toward downtown. At 11:45 on a Friday morning, I-64 would be maxed out with everything imaginable: cars, buses, motorcycles, SUVs, pick-ups, campers, delivery trucks, car carriers, loaded oil trucks, bulldozer haulers, double-hitched eighteen wheelers, horse trailers, and much more. Whatever was legal on the American road would be packed onto that forty-year-old highway at this peak-use hour, all doing sixty-four miles an hour since the speed limit was fifty-five, all in a frantic hurry to get wherever they were going since that's the way we Americans drive, and all frazzled by the hectic chaos. And this funeral director was going to dump another thirty cars into the mix. "You idiot!" I shouted. Of course, he couldn't hear me.

But, forward we went. Little did I know that the worst was to come. The entire line of us pointed down the entry ramp into I-64. Miracle! There was a brief opening, and seven or eight of us got in with little trouble. "Maybe the others will be lucky too," I thought, "and we'll gather once we get off the exit ramp." But then the totally bizarre happened. Leading our procession (I was second in line), the funeral home director settled us in at the somber, reverent, pious speed of twenty-eight miles per hour. "Funerals should be conducted in awe and dignity," I could hear him thinking, "and that includes the procession." We were going to proceed as if we were winding down an isolated country road.

In the lane to our left, fifty-thousand-pound masses of steel were hurtling past us at twice our speed. I was in my Volkswagen Beetle. The worst terror occurred when I glanced in the rearview mirror. Giant hulks were angling left, angling right, straining with every braking power they possessed to miss this snail-paced impediment. A chaotic pile-up had not yet happened but was on the verge.

I hit my headlights, on, off, on, off, on, off: "Move!" We maintained twenty-eight miles per hour.

I waved frantically with arms and head: "Pick it up! Get going, you imbecile!" Twenty-eight miles per hour.

I went to the horn, three times, five times, seven times. "You're going to need a dozen funerals after this insanity, you fool! Move!" Twenty-eight miles per hour. No budge.

I prayed. I gasped. My nerves clanged. My senses went berserk. Moment by moment, I anticipated catastrophe. But, miraculously, nothing happened, except for incensed, snarling drivers whizzing by on our left. Two miles, three miles, four miles down the interstate we went. Then we approached the lengthy I-64 tunnel, even more narrow, with no space on either side. "Oh, God, get us through here without an inferno." Twenty-eight miles per hour.

Beyond the tunnel, we veered onto the Grinstead Drive exit. It had never occurred to me that descending an interstate ramp could be filled with exhilarating joy. Three, four, five, six cars behind us, they were all making it off. We turned onto Grinstead Drive and paused to let all twenty-eight cars catch up. I was drained, emptied. We drove a half mile and turned into the cemetery gate. We were suddenly surrounded by a great calm, gorgeous old trees and quiet, stately tombstones, a magnificent sight!

The three funeral home limousines behind me had all carried family members. Arriving at the grave site, I had exactly fifteen seconds to recover myself and relate warmly to everyone. Preachers have to get good at that: The families had been in the back seats of the funeral home limos and would be much less aware of what had happened.

We held the committal service at the grave. No surprises, everything normal.

When most folks had left, the funeral home director eased over toward where I stood, obviously to have a needed conversation.

"Will you tell me what you were thinking out there?" I asked in the most friendly and non-critical voice I could muster. "I don't get it."

His reply was terse, "This is a holy event. God wouldn't let anything happen to us out there."

"Your religion almost killed a dozen people. I don't think God protects us against our own foolishness."

"You need a stronger faith," he retorted.

"Enough! Stop there!" I said to myself. "He's a fundamentally pleasant, mostly competent man, and I'll be working with him on future occasions. There's no need in building walls." I shook his hand, turned, and walked away, vowing that next time I would take my own route to the cemetery. A red Volkswagen Beetle at the head of a funeral procession looks a little strange anyway.

23

Death of an Era

A FTER THE service was complete, I walked down a long hallway of the funeral home headed toward my car. Three young
men stood talking in the hallway. I didn't know them. They were
lawyer friends of my cousin, Adam. They all looked promising,
self-confident, assertive, as if a piece of the future belonged to
them, and they knew it.

"Pardon me. Are you a family member?" one asked.

"Yes, I'm Adam's cousin."

"Well, maybe you can help us understand. Why would Mr.
Fisher do a thing like this? He was a pleasant, friendly man, very
nice. People liked him. He had lots of good years left; how old was
he, late fifties? It was such a waste. Why would he take his own life?
Do you know?"

Yes, I knew. Uncle Red had graduated from high school in
1928. As with many in his generation, he did not go to college. He
found work with Interstate Milling Company in Charlotte, North
Carolina. He worked in the distribution warehouse, receiving
packages of flour from the company mill and arranging them for
shipment to grocery stores across North and South Carolina. It
was an "entry level job," which in Uncle Red's time meant that if he
worked hard, showed ability, and was faithful, he might well "climb
the ladder," as it was said.

Uncle Red lived by the script. After two or three years of good work, he was advanced. A decade later, when the warehouse manager retired, Mr. and Mrs. Clement, the company owners, asked Uncle Red to take over. He labored in that role for nearly a quarter century, relating closely with Mr. Clement who ran the entire business. Uncle Red was a devoted disciple. If night work was needed, he worked nights. If weekend, weekends. He adapted to the changing markets and came to read Mr. Clement's mind in making decisions. Most of all, Uncle Red was on first name terms with virtually every client in their distribution network. He knew who liked what how, and he made special arrangements to maintain the retailers' loyalty. Interstate Milling flour appeared on grocery shelves across a wide geographical expanse, and Uncle Red devoted himself to keeping it that way.

Because of their cultural and economic differences, Uncle Red and Mr. Clement were never social friends, but in the warehouse office they were hand-in-glove.

Then the day came when Mr. Clement died. Shock waves swept through the company, but Uncle Red and others rose to the task. They began relating with Mrs. Clement in keeping the company strong—she had never been much involved before. With the dependable devotion of the several supervisors, they kept going for another decade.

Then Mrs. Clement died. Their children, not interested in flour milling, had long since moved elsewhere. The decision was easy for them: liquidate.

They sold everything to a larger competitor. The buyer was expanding its company operations and modernizing its plants. An early casualty of the sale was Uncle Red. Who wanted a fifty-seven-year-old man from the past era? His personal relationships with the company's customers did not matter to the new corporate owner. This group believed that competitive cost was the key to selling the product.

In a short time, Uncle Red was without work and income. There was a pension, but it did not come near his former salary. More importantly, he lost his identity, his sense of who he was. You could see it in his demeanor, an aimless wandering, but even more in his eyes: vacant.

He looked for another job. His brother-in-law, Tom, a hundred miles away, finally offered him work in the small trucking company that Tom owned and operated. Uncle Red and his wife moved the hundred miles, and he tried it. But his work did not go well. Uncle Red was not an asset in the trucking business.

Thus, one day, Uncle Red got in his car, drove out to a large lake on Tom's residential property, parked, arranged his car keys, wallet, and watch carefully on the front seat, and drowned himself in the lake. It was one of those horrible events that leave everyone numb and lifeless, but in retrospect no one could say that it was a surprise.

Should Uncle Red have been able to reinvent himself? It's easy to look back and tell him what he should have done. Not long after Uncle Red's death, I was sitting in a doctor's office waiting room reading a magazine article on *the future's successful employee.* "You've got to market yourself!" the article counseled. "Tomorrow's most valued employee will be the one who is always looking for something better, constantly honing his or her image as a desirable commodity. You will do best if your boss is always a bit wary that you might leave." Uncle Red would have been lost in that world. His asset was loyalty, and in his day it worked both ways.

Should the buyers of Interstate Milling Company have placed a higher value on this near-retirement man who had worked diligently in the company's best interests for thirty-eight years? Buy-up companies see themselves as purchasing assets and shedding liabilities, and I doubt that one Master of Business Administration program in a thousand teaches a moral obligation to find a role for old, used-up employees.

That day, we were holding a funeral not just for Uncle Red but for an entire era in American life. He was a casualty of the shift from family industry to corporate America, from a personal relationship among individuals with names to high-efficiency, faceless mass operation, from mutual fidelity to "you're-on-your-own." It was a seismic transformation sweeping America in the middle decades of the twentieth century, and Uncle Red was one of its many victims.

"Why would Mr. Fisher have done this?" Is it possible for young men with sparkling educations and a world of opportunity before them to understand why? Perhaps not, unless your own father had had the same experience. I replied, "The company where he worked for almost four decades was modernizing and didn't want him around any longer." The young men seemed to understand but quickly turned away, ending the conversation, as if they didn't want to hear more. I found that strange until I realized that they might soon be counseling big-business America on how legally to dispose of the Uncle Reds of the world. They could not allow his emotional world to take up residence in their consciousness, even if he was Adam's father. Life has to move forward, you know.

24

Saying Goodbye to Albert

ALBERT NIFONG (Bert) was a clinical psychologist who specialized in adolescents. A full schedule of youngsters came to him for treatment. He tended the most fragile, seeking to equip disturbed and wounded kids in making their way successfully into the future. It was hard work, but he was good at it, having built a reputation for his effectiveness. More than a few young people and their parents had seen the value of his work.

Albert's wife, Charlene, a pharmacist, came home from work one day for lunch. On her phone machine was a message that Bert was not in his office. He had worked half the morning calendar, had gone out for a break, and had not come back. His receptionist was wondering if Charlene knew where he was. Sometimes during racing season he would spend half a day at the Downs. The office was wondering if he had given any hint that he might be going there. With scant concern, Charlene went down to the basement to change some clothes from the washer to the dryer.

Descending the steps, she suddenly was aware of two legs and feet dangling in the air beside her right shoulder. She froze, then shrieked in disbelief, and, sobbing, fainted on the steps. Albert had come home, tied a noose around his neck, looped the rope over a water pipe, and stepped off the side of the staircase.

The full drama followed. Police came. The emergency medical service arrived. The medical examiner, concerned neighbors, a newspaper reporter, psychologist and pharmacy colleagues, pastors, church friends, and schoolmates of their two teenage children all came. The next three days was a stream of visitors and emotions.

The funeral was one large question mark: why would Dr. Nifong have done this? The people who had seen him lately had not sensed any danger signs. Psychologists, a lot of people thought, were supposed to have themselves pretty well together, and this just didn't fit. Suicides drown everyone in unanswered questions.

After the funeral, Charlene began to see me. From the beginning, she was filled with remorse, endlessly reviewing all the ways she might have prevented it, and blaming herself for not doing so.

Bert had been a very competent psychologist with a good practice, she said. His reputation had been well earned, and his fans were many. But Bert was never able to apply his therapy to himself. Charlene told me that after he got home at night, he sometimes suffered acute anxiety: what might happen with this client or that, whether his clients might discover that he was the fraud he suspected he was, whether someone would sue him for malpractice, whether he might experience a dramatic drop in business due to some error, and what his psychologist peers thought of him. Too many evenings Bert had occupied with his fretting, enough that Charlene had come mostly to discount it as Bert's eternal battle within himself. "At times, his insecurities could turn him into a pathetic little boy searching for a safe place on his mother's lap. I grew sick of being asked to be my husband's mother.

"Maybe that's why you become a psychologist," she said, "to try to heal yourself. Bert never did. His techniques worked great at the office, but they crashed and burned when he walked in our front door. He carefully guarded his anxious underside from public view, believing that any hint would destroy him.

"And then there was the other matter," said Charlene, rolling her eyes in deep disgust and anger. "Those trips to the Downs were part of something much larger. I discovered after Bert killed himself that there were several hundred-thousand dollars we no longer possessed. Between our two salaries, we had saved for more than a decade, for educations, for the future. I thought we were doing pretty well. Gone! All of it! Bert had a gambling addiction. The Downs was only the beginning. There were college football games, lotteries, slots, and casinos. He carried on all of it at his office, and I had no more than a couple of small hints. Those damned gambling people loved him, courted him, always found some splendid new opportunity for him. They knew red meat when they saw it, and they ate Bert alive. I could kill the lot of them! Where are they now? 'Oh, we never had much association with him,' they claimed. 'He placed a bet now and then, but that was all.' They are a pack of greedy, exploitative, lying bastards.

"All of this saga, of course, was interlaced with our precious child, Amy. Our son, Rob, is mostly just a normal fifteen-year-old who does fine. But older sister, Amy, was born to push the envelope. From day-one, she didn't believe the rules apply to her. She does things the way she damned well pleases. Amy tolerates her parents only because we feed her and provide money, but she mostly wants to be out somewhere having fun. We live with a time bomb.

"Bert was helpless with Amy, barely a father, not at all a therapist. Here is his own child living directly in his vision every day, and all of his theories, models, and treatments had no effect. I think he and she were too much alike, both searching for something they missed in their make-ups, and neither able to resolve it."

As Charlene was talking, I, myself, recalled the Sunday morning I had asked Albert to lead a Sunday school class at Highland Church on "communicating with your teenager." He had addressed an overflow crowd about active listening, non-judgmental empathy, entry into their mental worlds, and expressing consequences, not condemnations. Bert had done a marvelous teaching job. When the hour ended, enthusiastic applause followed and a jam of people crowded around him. Charlene, sitting next to my wife, Nancy, commented quietly, "It's too bad he can't make any of that shit work at home."

"The most pathetic thing Bert could have done," Charlene said, "was bail out! Leave me with only one income to pay off our house and his gambling debts. And I also get Amy by myself now. How do I try to keep up with her and do my work too? Bert took the damned easy way out!

"And yet, I also loved the man. He could be kind and considerate, going out of his way to take me into account and be good to me. He could be funny as a comedian, making all of us laugh our silly heads off. In social settings, he did really well conversing with friends. And he didn't have any of the alcohol or other-woman problems some men have. I loved him most of all because of how much he loved me. Despite his difficulties, there was never a day when he didn't seem to put me at the top of his list. I basically made a good choice in marrying Bert."

Thus did Charlene paint the contradictions. "What a childish, self-centered act! I could kill him for thinking suicide would help anything! That's not how you dig your way out of a hole!" But also, "I could have spotted the signs of his gambling addiction. Truth was, I didn't want to. I could have insisted that he seek help. I could have told Bert more often what a wonderful man he was, how much I loved him. I didn't do nearly enough. When I search for causes, I find myself looking straight in the mirror. Why didn't I make things better while I had the chance? The chance is gone now."

Charlene told me this tale several times through. One day, we went out to Bert's grave at the cemetery and she went through the whole story again. She was spiraling into an emotional pit, depressed and getting no better. She still had her job and family, but she was dying inside. And she didn't trust any of Bert's psychologist friends enough to seek professional help. "Professional," she would scoff. "I've seen enough of what that means!"

Weeks stretched to six months. "In my job," Charlene told me, "you have to pay close attention all the time and get things right. There is no room for error when you're giving medicine to people. Either you're right, or you're in big trouble. I stand there working, but I never know when the ugly shadows will descend. I never know when my mind will take me back to that scene on the basement steps, thinking how different it all could have been. The worst time is deep at night; a good night's sleep just doesn't happen with me now. Daytime is little better.

"We were sitting at the breakfast table the other morning, and I must have been staring off into space. Seventeen-year-old Amy suddenly looked at me and said, 'Mom, what are you doing? Are you talking to Daddy again? Has he walked in here and sat himself at our breakfast table? It's got to stop, Mom! Daddy's gone. He left us. And he's been coming back around too much lately. You've got to tell Dad to f--- off and quit this visiting. We've got other things to be doing now, and so does he.' I was put off by Amy's crudeness, but I had to admit that she was right."

Finally, I, her pastor, decided I needed to do something decisive, but I didn't know what. I have never thought of myself as a therapist, and I had not the slightest idea what to do with a woman in deep depression. Lots of my seminary peers had specialized in the very popular field of pastoral counseling, but not I. My best recourse was to consult a psychologist friend.

I called a professor of clinical psychology whom I respected. I described the situation to him. I thought he would recommend that Charlene see him. He didn't.

"Try this," he said, describing an apparently well-known counseling technique. He gave me specific instructions and said that my lengthy relationship with Charlene would be important in giving it a chance to work. I came away with serious misgivings, but also hopeful.

I called Charlene. "When do you have an afternoon free this week?"

"Wednesday."

"Can we get together here at the church? I want to work through a process with you."

"I'll be there."

I chose a secluded, upper-floor room at the church. I placed five chairs in the room. With masking tape and index cards, I labeled the chairs "Jim," "Charlene," "Bert," "Herbie, the gambler," and "God." Having thus set up the room, I realized that I had become possessed by a very strong confidence that *this was going to work*. I didn't know where that feeling had come from. It certainly had no historical basis, but it was strong.

When he had first arrived at Warren Wilson College, our younger son, Will, had written a paper on "peak performance." Will had been a juggler in high school, and he had told of performing one Saturday morning with the Louisville Symphony Orchestra before eight hundred children and their parents. He had traveled to the show feverish with flu, not certain he could perform at all. But for the twenty minutes he and his cohort, Marcus Perry, were on stage, *absolutely nothing could go wrong*. They did their routine more perfectly than ever before, even using some sort of mental telepathy to improvise elaborations, all of which worked. The paper for college was on Will's state of mind during that experience, a burst of confidence that had created "peak performance." Peak performance is what I felt going into that afternoon with Charlene. Even though I had very little confidence in myself as a counselor, I knew this was going to work.

She arrived. We climbed the stairs to the upper room. I said, "Charlene, I'm going to sit in my chair, labeled 'Jim.' You sit in your 'Charlene' chair. Across from you, we are going to set 'Herbie, the gambler.' You are to talk to Herbie and say absolutely everything you have to say to him. Don't leave anything out. Don't soften it. You don't have to be polite."

Charlene rolled her eyes and looked extremely doubtful, but then said, "Well, I can't guarantee how this will come out, but I'll try.

"Herbie, I've never met you, so that I don't know you personally. But I do know that you are a pathetic, wretched, sorry-ass, self-centered bastard of a human being. My mother taught me that if I was going to say something about somebody, I should say the best thing I can. That's the best I can say about you. You have devoted your life to learning to manipulate vulnerable people. I've met some pretty low-grade swine, but you are at the bottom. You don't care about anyone but yourself. You say whatever words will work to get money for you, be it truth or lie. You play on people's weaknesses. You specialize in dragging down your fellow human beings." Charlene went on through five minutes of pure venom. I kept waiting for Herbie to materialize and slap her, but in her mood Charlene would have taken good care of herself.

"Okay," I said when she finished with Herbie, "now let's move Bert into position. Talk to Bert. Say *everything*. No holding back. I want Bert to hear it all."

"Bert, why the hell did you do this? Take off and leave me! We promised each other, 'in joy and in sorrow, in plenty and in want, in sickness and in health.' What happened to your end of the bargain? I am thoroughly pissed at you and your poor-little-me behavior. Always thinking the sky was falling! Expecting the worst by tomorrow! You could be like a first grader scared of getting bullied at school. With all that education, you couldn't apply any of it to yourself. Your whole problem was created by your mind, in the head on your shoulders. You didn't have a problem with your clients or with your peers. People thought you were wonderful. But you kept dreaming up all that doomsday garbage and believing it. 'What if they do this? What if they do that?' *They* weren't going to do any of those things, but you could never believe it. I'd like to know who planted all that self-doubt in your head, Bert. Probably your mother. She was the biggest worry package I've ever met, and you never could rise above the inheritance.

"And then there was your gambling addiction! Why didn't you tell me, Bert?" Charlene was roaring now. "Why did you squander all our money before doing something? Why did you leave me and your children with nothing but bills to pay? Couldn't you see that you weren't going to win any of it back? Those bastards don't work that way, Bert! That's not why they're in business! They do exactly what they did: take some vulnerable wretch who has a few dollars and make sure his family ends up broke. Bert, you were stupid! That's their whole design. I thought you had more common sense!"

She sat in tears, overcome by emotion. Fortunately, I had brought along a box of tissues. She wiped her eyes, sobbed gently again, and then collected her thoughts.

"Bert, I loved you and still do. "I miss you so much! We had great times. I remember our trip to London, riding the subway and getting off at different stops just to see what was there. We tried white water rafting in Tennessee and almost died laughing. Picking cherries in Michigan, The Louvre in Paris, the Chinese village in Toronto: you knew how to have a good time with people, Bert, and I loved it. I remember the night you had a four-course meal delivered to us at the Texas Ranger baseball game in Dallas because you knew I was hungry and didn't like hot dogs. The only place I didn't want to go with you was to your crazy psychologist conventions. I tried that once in Denver, and never again! Too many weird people per square inch. The normal world is crazy enough.

"Are we ever going to get Amy's head straight? That rebellious streak in her won't quit. And now you've copped out on raising her and left me to do it all. Bert, what sort of wimp are you? She's your daughter, you know, cut mostly from your cloth, and I was depending on you."

Charlene carried on like this for well over half an hour, vacillating in emotions.

"Okay," I said, "now I want you to change chairs with Bert. You sit in his place and talk to Charlene. Respond to what she just said."

"Oh, you've got to be kidding!" She winced and shook her head. But then she moved. After thinking for a few moments, she began.

"Charlene, I'm sorry. Really sorry! I tried all my life to get rid of the junk in my head, but I never did. It was like a disease that swept over me. Take a pill! Drink a medicine! Do something to repulse the attack! Nothing worked. I hated that you had to be married to that. If I brought it up, you would disdain me and I would withdraw into myself, which was the worst of all.

"I spent all our money trying to win back my losses. My luck couldn't stay bad forever. It had to turn, and when it did, I would recoup and get out. I convinced myself, with a little help from Herbie, that that would happen. Charlene, please forgive me! I know I've done a horrible thing. The demons were screaming! Please understand!"

Charlene moved back over and sat in her own chair. "Always self-pity, Bert. Finally, that was the only game you knew. Couldn't you ever rise up, stand on your own two feet, and face the challenge? I thought that was the man I was marrying. I guess it was just my naïve dream."

Charlene looked down into her lap, disgusted with herself. "There I go again, blaming it all on Bert, asking him to be something he wasn't. Why couldn't I have been a little more understanding?"

"I have to thank you, Bert, for the time we had together. You were a kind, sweet, wonderful man, and I loved you. I thank you for working hard to get me through pharmacy school. You gave me a profession, and I'm forever grateful. I thank you for being the father of our children, the most thrilling thing I have ever been involved in. I love those two children more than anything else in the world, and I wouldn't have them without you. I thank you for being my friend. This loneliness is horrible, and even though our life together was not always a picnic, you made things meaningful and often charming for me. You were a devoted husband, and I will never forget that. Thank you!"

Back to Bert's chair. "Thank you, Charlene. Regardless of what I did, you are the love of my life."

I then put Charlene back in the "Charlene" chair and moved the "God" chair into position before her. "Now, talk to God," I said. Search your soul. Don't confine yourself to being nice and polite. God can handle anything you say."

Charlene had some traditional complaints with God. "If you're a loving God, the way they say, why do you let things happen this way? Why are some people drowned in anxiety? Why do we get addictions? Why is the world full of manipulative people? Why can't Amy be a normal, fun, cute teenage girl the way others are? Why do we kill ourselves and spread around all the torment that results? Why doesn't the life we experience match the love you are supposed to have for us?"

Then, Charlene said, "God, I'm worried about something. This question nags at me a lot. I've been taught ever since I was a little kid that if you commit suicide, you automatically go to hell. I can't say that I really believe that, but I don't fully disbelieve it either. A whole bunch of my relatives believed it. Is Bert burning in hell right now, getting paid off for all the havoc he left here? Should I be offering some kind of prayers that you will forgive him, pull him out of the fire and let him spend eternity in a better place? He was too good for that. I loved him too much, and I want you to do me that favor, if it's needed. I think about this especially when I'm in bed at night and I look over at the empty space beside me. What's happening with Bert right now? Where is he?"

God gave no direct answer.

Charlene then told God that she was doing her best to stay faithful, to believe everything she was supposed to believe, but how hard it was at times like this. She told God how much she needed help in being alone. She talked about the mental torment, asking God to give her strength. And she promised God that she would take the best care possible of the children.

As Charlene was finishing with God, I had an idea I hadn't thought of before. I asked Charlene to sit still and wait for me. I went down two floors to the church kitchen. Was it possible that I might find some bread and grape juice? The church used them frequently, but would we have any left from the last time? As I descended the stairs, I *knew* I was going to find them. The sense that everything would go right had built. I reached the kitchen, and, sure enough, there it was, a half bottle of grape juice in the refrigerator (normally locked, not today) and the end of a French bread loaf wrapped in plastic in a basket. I found three small glasses and saucers and carried it all upstairs.

Charlene and I started with prayer. I recited the Lord's Supper text from 1 Corinthians 11. I spoke a word about the meaning of the text, how this meal was an enactment of God's forgiving love for us even through our worst sinfulness. I broke the French bread into three chunks and put them on the saucers. I poured grape juice into the three glasses.

Handing two saucers of bread to Charlene, I said, "The words of Jesus: 'This is my body which is broken for you. Do this in remembrance of me.' You are an ordained church elder, Charlene. Please serve Bert." Though Charlene had served communion in our congregation many times, she had never previously served a dead person. It took her a moment to figure out what to do. She mimicked handing one saucer to Bert and set it on Bert's chair, keeping the other for herself.

Handing Charlene two glasses of grape juice, I said, "The words of Jesus: 'This is my blood which is poured out for you. Do this in remembrance of me.'"

Charlene placed a glass of juice on Bert's chair and kept one.

"Now, let's all eat the bread together." We ate. "And let's all drink Christ's cup together." We drank.

"Has God answered your question?" I asked.

Charlene raised her brow, blinked, and rubbed her head, as she often did in moments of new insight. "I guess so. 'This is my body broken for you.' It's not what Albert did that determines what happens to him. It's what Jesus did." She smiled a triumphant smile. The ancient and accustomed ritual of holy communion had come to life in a new way. We joined our hands and sat silently.

"Do you want to say anything else to anyone?" I asked.

Charlene thought for a moment. "Yes, I want to say one more thing to Bert."

Facing Bert's chair, Charlene said, "Bert, I love you. Despite what you did, I love you dearly. But there's one thing I need to ask you to do. Sitting here next to God, I guess I better not say it the way your daughter said it the other day, but I think she was right. It's time for you to stop showing up. You will always be in our hearts, and we'll hope to see you again, but for now your visits need to become less frequent. As Amy said, 'We've got other things to be doing, and so do you.'" Charlene then went on to speak her deepest love and farewell to her husband.

She smiled at me.

"We're through?" I asked.

"We're through."

I don't tend to be a deeply mystical person. I don't use candles, incense, or labyrinths; they hold no interest for me. But when I encounter The Holy in the intensity of the human struggle, I try to be aware of it. I remember no stronger encounter than this one.

The two of us arose and headed down the steps, three hours after we had begun. The three hours had been timeless, neither of us at all aware of the clock.

Before leaving, Charlene turned and sobbed on my shoulder, thanking me profoundly.

"I hope you have a really good weekend," I said.

"I expect to," she replied.

The church staff had left for the afternoon, and I was alone in the building. I proceeded back to the upper room to clean up.

As I climbed the steps, I was possessed by a very strange feeling. "What if Bert's bread and grape juice are gone? What if saucer and glass are empty?" I was nearly shaking in anticipation, not really thinking it was possible, but not sure. When I entered to room, the bread and juice were still there. No further miracle. One had been enough for that afternoon.

Three weeks later, I had a call. It was Charlene's best friend, Emily. "I don't know what you and Charlene did, because she hasn't talked much. But whatever it was, she is a new person. Back to being Charlene! She's joined us again. I want to thank you."

"You're welcome, Emily. Give me no credit. I was little more than a bystander. The things that happened were much bigger than both of us. You might call it a resurrection."

Thus it was: saying goodbye to Albert.

25

Nettie's Lure

NETTIE WAS an eighty-five-year-old widow in my church. She was very wealthy and had no children. She occupied a large house with her two sisters, one also a widow, the other never married. There were no children in the whole family complex, no next generation.

From my first visit with Nettie, I enjoyed a warm reception. All three sisters joined the lively conversation every time I went.

Nettie, however, was a bit too cordial. She appointed a place in her backyard where I could park, and she wanted me to use it often. "Stop on your way home from work, Jim. You don't have to call. We want you to bring your wife by sometime too. We'd like to know her. You just think of our house as your second home in this neighborhood. We've got this big center room we all share, and you are always welcome."

Before long, our phone started ringing. "Dorothy and I want you and Nancy to be our guests for dinner at The Club." The Club was a white-Protestant-only private organization that sprawled over half a city block downtown, the gated safe haven of the city's social elite. "We want you to do *this* with us; we'd like you to do *that* with us." Nettie seemed intent on pulling her pastor into her lifestyle, but also into her mind set. It was apparent early that there was quiet bribery attached to her benevolence: she wanted to get me thinking the way she did.

I had come to Highland Church because it was a strong congregation on the edge of downtown. Similar churches had long ago fled to the suburbs, following their members. Highland had stayed, weathering assorted member departures through the years. When I went there, I saw it as a strong, accomplished, aging, largely conservative congregation, a challenge, but a group of people fully capable of engaging with the dynamics of downtown. I had just spent seven years as an inner-city pastor, and I easily identified roles a congregation like this could play in the city's life. One outcome would be an intense eighteen year relationship with a near-downtown African-American church the same size as Highland, West Chestnut Street Baptist. We two congregations interwove our lives in multiple ways, holding periodic joint worship services and choir exchanges, sponsoring mixed dessert gatherings in member homes, participating together in an annual Ohio Riverbank clean-up, placing our members side-by-side in district courtrooms in the Court Education Project, sending seventy adult volunteers into the lowest scoring elementary school in the Jefferson County public system to read with young children, and holding hilariously fun church picnics together.

Nettie, however, wanted me to join her world. "Don't you agree with me that trying to work with all those *nigras* is a no-win idea? They just need to *go to work*, and then they won't be poor any longer. Don't you think that's right? All this marching is nothing but a group of lazies demanding what they don't deserve. If they'd do an honest day's work, they wouldn't have time to demonstrate. Don't you look at it that way?"

And Nettie always included her final appeal. She was prepared to leave a substantial amount of her wealth to Highland Presbyterian Church. She never said overtly that it was contingent on my following her bidding, but both of us understood that it was. *Never* did the hints not come. "Jim, that vase over there is worth a lot of money, and I'm thinking of making it one of the things I leave to the church when I die." I could be a highly success-ful pastor with no financial worries if I would work to maintain her church as a religious version of The Club.

I related to Nettie as with other church members, visiting her periodically and carrying on a cordial friendship, but never adjusting my beliefs or my church leadership to her agenda. And never accepting dinner at The Club. We had gone there once with two other couples, and that was more than enough (women were required to enter through a side door, which was only the beginning).

When Nettie died, we held her funeral. Friends came to cel-ebrate her life and God's love. Only I knew the underlying drama. She left not a penny to Highland Presbyterian Church. I was sorry but not surprised.

I discussed this story with several friends, seeking to know if there was a better way I could have handled it. Especially en-lightening were the words of a retired seminary president who has done plenty of fund raising while maintaining the academic integrity of his school.

"I'd bet that in your conversations with her you never faced the issue head-on. Is that right? You circled around it with both of you knowing what you were talking about but neither of you addressing it directly."

"You're exactly right," I acknowledged.

"Jim. you're from the South, and so am I. That's the way we do things here, always remaining oblique so as not to confront or offend. I did that for years. I wonder what would have happened if you had said to her, 'Nettie, you have your ideas for Highland Church, and you really believe in them. I have different ideas, and I believe in mine too. I think it's wonderful that you and I can be friends, pastor and member, even though we have different no-tions. I hope you will leave a nice bequest to the church, because we need it. We will do valuable things with your money, such as refurbishing the building used by children in the weekday school, or hiring the staff to carry on an active ministry among older members of the church. We need you to help with those things, even though you and I don't agree on what the church is doing downtown.'"

I wish I had tried my friend's suggestion. Maybe I was too timid, or too stubborn.

I also know, however, that our nearly two-decade relationship with West Chestnut Street Baptist provided rich rewards for both congregations and for the whole city, and that no amount of money could match that. The relationship was non-negotiable. The most critical possession of any pastor is his/her convictions. If those are for sale, then the pastor is not leading anyone anywhere worth going.

26

Sagacious Old Man

GEORGE WHITE was a retired medical doctor, eighty-six, a friend and church member. He was a quiet man, hardly noticeable. George cherished "old time values," the straightforward, right-and-wrong thinking taught him from his birth. This sometimes set him apart from me, but I had long ago learned that when George spoke, I wanted to listen. He did not use words lightly. Beneath his introspective exterior was a lifetime of experience and insight. Agree with him or not, I found him a keen observer of human life. That's why I made an appointment to have lunch with him on a particular day.

I began the conversation. "George, you've got the most expressive granddaughter I've ever seen," referring to six-year-old Evan. Evan was special! Singing in our youngest children's choir, she repeatedly commanded center stage, not because of her singing voice but because her face was an open book. Everywhere she went, in everything she did, Evan beamed what she was thinking in full clarity. Excitement, joy, trepidation, uncertainty, determination, or dismay, it all shone brightly. The congregation had been magnetically drawn to watching Evan. "I would love to have a camera to catch all the moods on that child's face," I said to George. "She is one hundred percent authentic."

George beamed. "Yes, Evan is a joy! I love being with her. She and her mother have me over for dinner every Wednesday night, and I always look forward to it."

George's wife had died several years before. She had been their social calendar motivator, as gregarious as George was an introvert. With her gone, however, George had known he needed to take new initiative. Sitting at home was not good. He needed to make himself get out with people.

"Where does Evan go to school?" I asked.

"The Brown School," he replied. Brown School was downtown. It purposely drew students from every part of the city and county. It was as racially, economically, and culturally desegregated as its dedicated leaders could make it. It ranked diversity among its highest values, wanting its students to learn to relate to the world of their future. Both our sons had attended there.

"That's a good school," I said.

"Yes," George replied, "it is. But with all the different friends Evan has made, I have to be careful. She has white friends, black friends, brown friends, every color. She doesn't attach any special meaning to that. To her, they are all just friends. My attitudes come from an age long past. I can't get beyond them. But I have to be careful not to pass my thinking on to her. I have to watch what I say, because she picks up everything."

George then went on to relate a piece of his history. "My father was a doctor too. He had his office on West Main Street in Louisville. Early in his practice, he had patients both white and black. They came to his office at the same time. But the white people didn't like sitting in the same waiting room with black people, so that pretty soon all his patients were black. He loved them, and they loved him; he served them well.

"But I don't ever remember feeling that he thought of them as his equal. I grew up believing they were not as smart, not as culturally advanced, not quite as moral as we were. No one ever said that. It was just implied.

"Recently, I read Colin Powell's book. He is one smart man. He knew how to look at big pictures and have large agendas. I was really impressed. The book began changing the way I think about his race. If Colin Powell can be that intelligent, there must be many others. I'm trying to take on this new attitude, but it's hard to get rid of the old one. It's deep in me.

"And that's what I've got to be careful about with Evan: the little comments I make. She doesn't need Granddaddy's old-time way of thinking. She needs to set her own path. It's a new world, and my attitudes won't help her."

"Dr. White," I thought to myself, "You are a man of great wisdom. I disagree with you on some things, but I respect deeply your self-perception. Evan is fortunate to have you as her granddaddy."

One of the things George White got himself out of the house to do was attend a lay Bible course I led at Louisville Presbyterian Seminary. He and Phyllis had come for several years, and he continued after her death. Not long after our lunch date, I was teaching a class on how God, all across Scripture, repeatedly moves beyond the boundaries of our human expectations and does things that startle and shock us. "God is always bigger than we think," I said. "Our minds are too small to predict what God will do next, and we need continually to struggle to keep up." George White was my perfect illustration: a man who related warmly to his granddaughter but who had the wisdom not to want to lock her in his past world. I told his story and expressed my profound appreciation.

Sitting at the same classroom table with George was a younger man named Scotty. Scotty told me later that George was beaming after the class, that several people came to him to pat him on the back and thank him for his example. His story was their story, they told him, and they appreciated the reinforcement.

George White died the next morning.

I told this entire account at his funeral. The outpouring continued. In the words of one person, "I am George. I love those little ones, but their world is completely different from mine. I find myself wanting to lecture them. 'Cool it, Grandma,' I say to myself. 'You're not here to raise them in your past. You are here to love them in their present.' I'm indebted to George."

27

The Southbrook Saga

IT WAS late afternoon, the time of day when nothing else is supposed to happen. Sun dropping, people's minds dropping, time to go home.

There was a tap on my office door. "Come in." It was Sammy Southbrook, a dark-haired, twenty-three-year-old who sometimes played in the outfield on our church softball team. "Come in, Sammy." He greeted me from the doorway and seated himself in a chair. Sammy was a good-looking guy: alert eyes, handsome features, a pleasant look, as long as he wasn't talking about his mother. I got no advance warning on what was coming. "Dr. Chatham, I'm dying of AIDS."

"Sammy!" I jolted. "You don't look like you're dying of anything," my mind thought. "That deceptive, cruel disease! How vicious can it get?"

"The final test result came back this morning," he said. "I've known for a while that something has been wrong, and this confirmed it. Dr. Gaddy gave me a complete physical, and there it was. Dr. Gaddy sent me to Dr. Marquis, the hematologist. Dr. Marquis consulted with Dr. Pettit and Dr. Tilley. They are in the immunology clinic at University Hospital. They examined all my test results and say I'm rapidly losing all my capacity to fight off disease, that if I get flu or even a cold, I may die."

It was late in the 1980s, still early in the AIDS advance, and both diagnosis and treatment were primitive.

"Sammy, that's horrible! You must be going through hell in your mind." He looked amazingly calm. Maybe he was just numb, moving mechanically and hiding the full reality from his own emotions.

"Dr. Pettit and Dr. Tilley are consulting with Dr. Edmund Johnston at the Boston Clinic. Dr. Johnston is a national specialist on AIDS. They are trying to find something that will prolong my life at least for a while. They told me to avoid contact with crowds, not to shake hands with anyone, not to have any physical contact, in part to protect them but mostly to protect me. That's pretty hard on a fun-loving, good-time guy like me. I'm big on relating to my friends and doing things. Now I have to keep a distance. But I can do it. It's better than spending the last weeks of my life in a hospital."

"Sammy, I am really sorry! What can I do to support you?"

"Pray for me, Dr. Chatham. I need your prayers. You're good at praying. It will help me to know you're doing it. Pray for me as much as you can."

"Sammy, I will pray for you many times. Whenever you think about it, I'll be praying for you."

"Thank you, Dr. Chatham. That's what I came here to ask. It will mean a lot." We had a prayer together, and Sammy left, saying he had to go back by the clinic before it closed for the day.

The following morning, I arrived at the church and was greeted by the bookkeeper, Harriet. "What's Sammy dying of this year?" she asked. I sagged in disbelief. "Last time it was leukemia. Ever since he was a teenager, he's been dying of something every two or three years. What is it now" I couldn't believe I had fallen for it.

Sammy came to me the next day for one more talk. He gave me another in-depth description of his terrible plight, doctors' names, medical test names, and all details. I listened. It was the last time I would hear from him for three years. The next time, he would be dying of hepatitis C.

Several years later, my new pastor colleague, Elizabeth, a bright, young business graduate from Indiana University and then from seminary, intercepted me one day in the office hallway, genuine concern written deeply in her eyes. "Jim, I have horrible news. We have a church member who is desperately sick, dying of lymphoma. A young man not yet thirty-five. I've spent the whole morning listening to his story."

"So, you met Sammy, did you?"

Pause. Wide eyes. Disbelief. Red face. "Oh, noooo! Don't tell me!"

"Join the multitude, Liz." That was the beginning.

A few years later, Sammy's father, Toby Southbrook, became ill. Retired now, Toby had been confined for several years to a wheelchair. In his healthier years, Toby had been a church usher, one of the fraternity of men who stood at the back of the sanctuary on Sunday mornings making sure arriving worshipers received bulletins. They often carried on rich personal relationships with one another.

The story was told that one Sunday morning Sammy came to church, which he seldom did. He eased quietly inside, took a bulletin, and then sat on the floor in a back corner of the sanctuary, wrapping himself in a nearly fetal position. Despite the efforts of his father and others, he stayed there through the whole worship hour. Toby had expressed to his cohorts frustration over his son, remarking that he had tried many times to bring Sammy to church. When asked gently, "How did Sammy get the way he is?" Toby had replied, "Have you ever met his mother?" I understood why Toby wanted to be an usher.

My first introduction to Mom had been years before in a phone call. Sammy had been about ten. "Reverend Chatham," an irritated female voice had addressed me, "This is Sara Southbrook. I am sitting in a chair in my living room looking out the front window. My neighbor, Mrs. Grimaldi, has just come out the front door of her house, and she is walking across the street toward my house. 'Walking' is the wrong word. 'Storming' would be better. Mrs. Grimaldi is very angry. She is coming to tell me that my son, Sammy, is a horrible playmate for her little boy, Ambrose. Ambrose is an anemic little thing, hardly able to fend for himself at all, and Sammy picks on him when the play together. Ambrose always ends up crying and running to his mother. Mrs. Grimaldi is correct. I have watched the two play, and Sammy is merciless toward Ambrose.

"I am calling because I want you, Dr. Chatham, to know that if our church had taught my son to behave himself as a Christian young man, taught him to treat people with respect, especially people who need pity the way poor little Ambrose does, I wouldn't be facing Mrs. Girmaldi's anger right now. I place the blame squarely on you for not having done better with my son. It's pathetic and shameful that God's church, which is supposed to teach children love and good behavior, abrogated its responsibility. When I was growing up, that never would have happened. They told us how we were supposed to act and what was going to happen if we didn't. All you people do now is let the children run off in any direction they want and turn into whatever they wish. I hope you are ashamed of yourself, Dr. Chatham, because you ought to be." With that, I heard the Southbrook doorbell ring, and we were finished.

Future calls were more generous, fortunately. Mrs. Southbrook apparently had a short memory.

Toby Southbrook passed away. It was a gentle death, in the deep of night. The Southbrook family gathered from near and far: a son from Charlotte who was a banker, with his wife and three children, a daughter from Des Moines who operated five candy stores, with her husband and two children, and another daughter from Pittsburgh. They inquired if I could meet with them the day before the funeral. I told them I would be very happy to do that, and that it would help me.

Arriving at the Southbrook home, I was greeted warmly. Young and old were gathered, all the way down to Toby's ten-year-old granddaughter. I was made to feel like a genuine family friend. Sammy's mother was winningly gracious.

The first thing obvious, however, was: no Sammy. I had to admit that I was relieved that neither I nor the family would spend two hours hearing about his Lou Gehrig's disease. But I also regretted his absence. Sammy belonged; he was part of the family. How could they omit him? I suspected we would pay a price for this. It wasn't, however, for me to control.

I asked each person to describe his and her major image of Toby. "How will you remember him? What are the best stories you have to tell about you and him? How did he influence you?" Adults and children all contributed, drawing a life-size portrait of Toby Southbrook.

"Daddy worked for Hobson-Atkins Construction Company. Did all the ordering and stocking. He was constantly keeping up with who was going to need what and at which construction site, and then he'd be on the phone ordering a train car load of concrete blocks, or ten thousand two-by-fours, or a truck full of plywood, or five hundred kegs of nails, always huge amounts. The most expensive thing his company could do was have a work crew delayed for several hours because they ran out of supplies. Daddy's job was to make sure that didn't happen. He bought in such large quantities that the suppliers courted him. We got some really nice gifts: TV sets, microwaves. We once went to the Bahamas because Daddy had out-bought from one supplier every other construction company east of the Mississippi. It was a great vacation."

"Daddy collected rocks. Gathered them from all over the world. Red rocks, blue rocks, silver rocks, volcano rocks, ancient rocks. He had a fascination. He became an officer in the local rock collecting society. Went to their meetings once each month, never missed. He loved those guys. They'd sit there all night and carry on about their rocks. He tried to take us, but none of us was ever interested. He finally got the message and just went by himself."

"Also cats. Daddy never saw a cat he didn't love. Any lame old stray, emaciated and hungry, looking for a meal and a place to stay, all he needed to do was meow at Daddy. He knew all the varieties, all the habits, all the peculiarities. A cat could walk into a room with ten people sitting there, and the cat would walk over and jump up on Daddy's lap because he knew instinctively who would love him. Daddy used to build ledges up high around our walls so the cats could sit up there, the way they like to do. Also seats on the window sills so they could gaze outside. There have been times when twelve cats at one time called his place home. They'd wander through day and night, just hanging around."

"And church ushering. He loved church ushering. Morris Clevenger, Joe Sparks, Charlie Ward, Edgar Baumeister, and Cyril Pfingst: they were his friends, and he couldn't wait to see them on Sundays. Daddy would be the first out of here."

"And then there was the Navy. He served in World War II, a sailor on a destroyer. A closer group of friends he never made in his life. They met somewhere every year to remember old times. Manson Ray, Eddie Benedict, Orvis Lee, and Omar Poole—we heard so much about them, I still remember their names. Daddy never got over being in the Navy, and there was nothing in his life he was more proud of."

"I think Daddy was the finest father we could have had. He loved us. He took interest in each of us individually. He was always there when we needed him. He was warm, funny, serious. I always knew I had a Daddy who cared deeply about my life, and I can't ask for any more than that. I'd like to place a big 'number one' sticker on his coat lapel."

There was a pause. The children seemed to have completed their superlatives. They had certainly spoken admirably. Sara Southbrook hadn't said much, but here she injected herself. "We have to admit, as well, that Toby could out-drink a dozen other men. He could down a fifth of bourbon in one sitting, straight. Never drank in public, but he could sure pack it away in our kitchen. I used to wonder why he didn't burn out his insides. Must have learned it in the Navy. Thank God, he didn't get violent the way some men do. Toby just got more mellow, glazed, happy. Well into his second bottle, I wasn't sure he knew who even his wife was. Finally, I'd just lock the cabinets, which was the only way to make him stop. When he couldn't find any more, he would ease off to bed and go to sleep."

"Aw, Mama, com'on now, we don't want to put all that old stuff in his funeral," one of the children complained.

"Well, why not? We want a real picture, don't we?" Sara replied. "Your Daddy had some good things about him, and he had some bad things about him, and we want to tell the whole story, don't we?" No one in the room knew how to stop her.

"The term 'curses like a sailor' originated with Toby. He could be so vile in his language that you just didn't want to hear it! Nasty, filthy words! He knew more than the whole dictionary. That man could curse the world, curse the weather, curse some supplier who had not delivered, curse his bosses, curse the government, curse some driver who pulled out in front of him. He could turn a winter night hot. Toby cursed more than any other human being I've ever known. I just hope the good Lord has gotten a little deaf in his old age.

"Reverend Chatham, let me show you Toby's scrapbook from the Navy." Mrs. Southbrook sprung to her feet and disappeared into the center hallway. Moments later, she came back toting a sizable scrapbook. "Just look at this, and you'll see how much Toby loved being in the Navy."

I opened the cover and was greeted by a full page black-and-white photograph. Young Toby stood in the center in a sailor suit on the deck of a ship. His left arm was draped over the shoulders of another sailor, Richard Decker, whom Sara identified as his best pal. His right arm was coiled around the body of a very attractive young nurse. She appeared to be in no hurry to unleash herself.

After nearly two hours, I had my picture. With this, and with what I already knew about Toby, I could speak a fitting portrayal. The family would feel good, and we could honor the man's life.

That night, my phone rang at home. It was Sammy. "Dr. Chatham, I know you met with my family this afternoon. They did not want me to come because they felt I might be too disruptive. I wouldn't have been disruptive at all, but they didn't trust me. I'm calling because I want to speak at my father's funeral tomorrow. There are some things I want to say, and I didn't get to say anything this afternoon. I'll say them at the funeral. You call on me."

"Sammy," I said, "we'll need to check with your Mom. If she say's it's okay for you to speak, then you're welcome to speak. I'll call her in the morning and find out."

"Okay," Sammy replied. "I'm sure she'll say yes." I, myself, fully expected her to say no.

But Sammy was right. He would speak. Sara seemed to find no problem. Maybe she knew something I didn't know.

The funeral was held at Cave Hill Cemetery. A large tent had been erected. Chairs for fifty people were in place. Numerous people stood close to support Toby's family.

I saw Sammy beforehand and told him he was to speak, that I would call him forward. He had already gotten the word from his mother.

I said my remarks, leading a fairly standard funeral liturgy and painting my portrait of Toby. I then said, "Sammy Southbrook, Toby's son, would like to speak to us." There was nothing unusual about this. Children of the deceased often speak at funerals.

Sammy stepped forward and faced the gathering. Normally, I would have sat down in the front row of chairs and become part of his audience. This time, I decided to stay where I was, just behind Sammy's left shoulder.

Sammy began. "From my Mom and my brother and sisters and me, I want to thank you all for coming here today. It means a lot to us that you want to be with us in Dad's funeral, to give us your support. We will never forget it.

"He was a good man, someone I loved deeply and looked up to. I don't know how God could have given me and Evelyn and Anna and Christopher a better father. He did everything we could have asked and far more. We will thank him forever." I had known that Sammy was articulate, but I had never heard him before an audience. He looked directly at them and very quickly owned the place.

"Some of you here were my father's special friends, and you were wonderful to him. Edwin Crews, right over there; hold up your hand, Mr. Crews. Edwin Crews was Daddy's work companion. They labored together at Hobson-Atkins for years, and there was no one Daddy trusted and respected more than you, Mr. Crews. You were a dependable friend, especially when Daddy needed one most. I want to thank you for who you were and what you did; it will always mean a lot to our family.

"Charles Potter, over there. Mr. Potter used to go fishing with Daddy. They could talk and tell stories all day long. Daddy would come home beaming with happiness after fishing with Mr. Potter, less because of the fish he had caught than because of the conversation they had had. Mr. Potter, on behalf of our family, I want to thank you for the friend you were to my Daddy. We count you as our friend too.

"Joe Crutchfield, right there. Mr. Crutchfield was in Daddy's rock club. He considered you the foremost expert. If there was something Daddy didn't know, he turned to you as his authority. Daddy loved and respected you. He used to tell us that Joe Crutchfield was the glue that held the club together, the main man who drew everyone else in. Joe Crutchfield, I thank you for the part you played in Daddy's life. I hope you hold your head high and feel proud of what you did.

"And Cyril Pfingst, a church usher with Dad. Dad liked your train stories, Mr. Pfingst, repeated them at our dinner table. He thought you treated people really well, and he wanted to be the kind of person you are."

Sammy made his way through five or six of Toby's friendships. I stood there in absolute awe. I had never, anywhere, heard a finer funeral oration from a family member. Sammy had to have been present and paying attention through years of family life to do what he had just done. And he obviously knew his father well: a man whose most valuable possessions in life were his personal friendships. Beginning in the Navy and extending to the present, these relationships were Toby's treasure, and Sammy brought that out beautifully. I had known that this young man bordered on brilliance, but I had never seen it at work this way.

Then he paused and scanned the gathering. "Now, there were some others of you here who weren't so nice to Dad, people who said things that hurt him or did things he thought were wrong."

I jerked to attention. The moment had come! I stepped forward and put my hand on Sammy's shoulder. He had talked seven or eight minutes already, easily enough. He turned and looked at me. I said, "Sammy, I need to move us forward."

"But I'm not through, Reverend Chatham. There's more I want to say."

"Sammy, you have made a wonderful statement. Everyone appreciates it. But some of them have been standing a good while, and we need to finish."

"But!"

"Sammy."

I knew the gathering was with me, but I wasn't sure I could stop him.

"Reverend Chatham wants me to stop. I'm not through, but I guess I have to do what he says."

Thank God, I had won.

"I do want those of you who were not kind to Daddy to re-alize that we know who you are, and that we don't forget these things." I tightened my grip on Sammy's shoulder. "Oh, yes, and one other thing. My father wasn't really a Presbyterian. For the first twenty years of his life, he was Catholic. He was raised in the Catholic Church, and the nuns and priests did a lot for him. We haven't even mentioned Daddy's Catholicism here today, so I brought this along." Sammy fished in his pocket and brought forth a small crucifix. "I wanted something that would honor my father's first religion." He walked over to the casket, bent to his knees, and dropped the crucifix under the casket into the vault. He got back up and said, "That crucifix will stay with him forever and will make him happy."

I looked at Sammy's sister, Evelyn, by now blue, red, purple, and about to explode.

"Thank you, Sammy, we appreciate what you have said. We know that you loved your father, and we thank you for telling us about it."

I concluded the service and invited those present to linger for conversation as long as they wished. I greeted family members one-by-one.

Ten minutes later, I realized that Evelyn and her husband were not in the group still lingering. They had gone out to their car and were sitting with the windows open. Knowing Evelyn fairly well, I walked out and put my elbows on the window ledge. "Are you okay?"

"Okay, except that I am mad as fury!" Evelyn replied. "I came out and got in the car so I could seethe in private."

"We almost had a mess on our hands," I said.

"Yeah, that's all we needed, Sammy standing up there peeling all the rotten apples. The second half of that speech would have burned the sky red, every strand of paranoia in Sammy's head.

"But what got me most was the crucifix. My Daddy despised his Catholic upbringing: too many strict nuns bullying him into conformity, too much self-righteous rigidity. He spent twelve years under that tyranny, and, once he escaped, he vowed never to associate with it another day. He used to say that they pounded enough guilt into him to last three lifetimes. He would be livid if he knew his casket was sitting on top of a crucifix. I'm furious at Sammy!

"But, don't worry! I'll have the final say! I have a friend who works on the crew here at the cemetery. I told him what happened, and he promised that after we're all gone, he will raise the casket, crawl underneath, and pull out the crucifix! Sammy won't know, but *I will!*"

Family! What more is there to say?

28

Rest, My Soul

THE MOUNTAIN town of Hindman, Kentucky, at least doubled in size that day. The state had lost one of its literary giants, and people came from all directions to pay their respects. The Hindman Funeral Services Chapel bulged, with more folks outside in the yard.

James Alexander Still had come to Knott County in 1932 to be the librarian at the Hindman Settlement School. He had lived there until his death in 2001. In his understated, minimalist style, he wrote novels, poetry, and children's literature that rank with the finest from the era. As a voice from "these prisoning hills," he told the world of the simple beauty and the stark tragedy of mountain life, the designs and the afflictions of nature, the endless struggles of a people to stay alive. A truck driver who once shared a Sunday evening meal with Mr. Still in a Somerset truck stop said as they parted, "Mister, you talk smart, but you got hillbilly wrote all over you." That is the clearest picture words can portray of this man.

Jim Still was born on Double Branch Farm just outside Lafayette, Alabama, in 1906, the oldest boy among ten siblings. His parents farmed, mostly cotton, and his father was a "horse doctor," a veterinarian without formal training. Still wrote his first story, "The Golden Nugget," at age eight or nine, the beginning of a lifelong devotion. In 1924 he became the first member of his family to enter college, Lincoln Memorial University in Cumberland Gap, Tennessee. He was assigned what turned out to be his dream student job, cleaning the campus library late at night. Many an evening, he tells us, after sweeping the floors, emptying the wastebaskets, and rubbing down the tables, he would drown himself in the several thousand books and magazines in the library's collection, often reading until daybreak.

Graduating from Lincoln Memorial in 1929, Still earned further degrees from Vanderbilt University and the University of Illinois. He was then offered a volunteer position at the Hindman Settlement School. During those lean years, no other offers came. The school promised food, shelter, and laundry, but no salary in return for his being their librarian. Three years later, they began paying him fifteen dollars per month. Publication of a few poems and short stories supplemented his income.

In 1939, Still moved his residence several miles to an old "log house," vintage 1827, on Dead Mare Branch Road facing Little Carr Creek. He went there to finish writing his novel, *River of Earth*, which had been contracted by Viking Press. He would make that log house his home until his death in 2001.

River of Earth, a work of captivating beauty in its warmth and pathos, depicts life in a coal mining family as told by the family's seven-year-old child. The migrations of the Baldridges in search of a place to settle, from farm to coal camp to farm to coal camp, tell of a mostly unseen American drama. The story parallels the travels of the Joad family in John Steinback's *The Grapes of Wrath*, with essentially the same unresolved outcome. In Still's characteristic style, River of Earth shows realities we don't really want to see in a way that leaves us wishing to see more.

James Still attended church often and was a friend of preachers (like me), but any sensing of his religion was hard to capture. I once tried to write a short statement on what I perceived, and found that almost everything was my conjecture. I guessed that, as a firm proponent of fewer words rather than more, Mr. Still found much religious proclamation to be verbal overkill, too much of the standard God, sin, and salvation talk and too little of the genuine quests of the human spirit, too many pat answers and not enough unanswerable questions. When he placed a sermon in the mouth of Brother Sim Mobberly in *River of Earth*, it resembled none at all the exhortations common to the pulpit but was the striving of a simple, hard-struggling mountain philosopher, "Where air we going on this mighty river of earth, a-borning, begetting, and a-dying? Where air it sweeping us?",[11] with no answers provided.

Still understood himself to be situated between the far reaches of eternity, a brief moment swept along by the flow of eons. The high mountains had once been valleys and would become so again; the valleys would rise to become mighty heights and sink again; thus was the ageless flow of River Earth. The creation in all its aspects was ever moving, never arriving at its destination. Humankind endlessly played out our accustomed plots. Love, beauty, self-sacrifice, prosperity, want, struggle, exploitation, revenge, violence, ingenuity, and stupidity: they all flowed in the endless river. "Where air we going?" Brother Mobberly asked. The question persists into our time with little resolution.

How do you best make a person's funeral reflect that person's life? The question is important to me. I have attended funerals in which the human being we buried barely resembled the one I had known. What should we do at Mr. Still's funeral to convey with integrity the man he was, rather than some mythic figure we might wish?

I read Psalm 90, which looks at life in the same way I understood James Still to look at it. Ancient Israel had just experienced the most wrenching event in its history (see Psalm 89), the destruction of Jerusalem and the overthrow of the Davidic monarchy by Babylon (587 BCE). According to Israel's faith, there was no way this could have happened! God was Jerusalem's

---

1. Still, James. *River of Earth* (Lexington: University of Kentucky, 1978), 76.

protector, David's guarantor, and the almighty Creator would keep that promise eternally! But it had happened. The city lay in ruins and the monarchy in the dust, with the best of Israel's citizens herded into exile. In the aftermath, Psalm 90 is a plaintive reflection on life's much larger perspective. "Lord, you have been our dwelling place in all generations. Before the mountains were brought forth, or ever you had formed the earth and the world, from everlasting to everlasting you are God (. . . .) A thousand years in your sight are like yesterday when it is past, or like a watch in the night" (vss 1–2, 4).

We humans live between everlasting and everlasting, a small instant in the vastness of God's foreverness. The psalm begs God, from the vantage of eternity, to give meaning into our struggling brevity. "Teach us to live our days with hearts of wisdom" (vs 12). We may not see destination, but can we at least know how to live well our allotted time? Can our days be spent in things that matter for good rather than in useless vanity? I think Mr. Still would have understood that quest.

I also read at the funeral Psalm 114, from which Brother Sim Mobberly had drawn his sermon text: "The mountains skipped like rams, the hills like lambs" (vs 4). Mobberly interpreted the psalm to mean that even the majestic heights and the sunken depths were moving vibrantly in the great flow of River Earth, all things traveling forward.

One early afternoon after Nancy and I had shared lunch with Mr. Still at the Settlement School, we drove out to his log house on Dead Mare Branch Road. We pulled into the dirt driveway. Mr. Still got out and walked toward the wooden gate into his property. He leaned on the gate rail, surveyed the farm yard before him, and spoke in a deeply genuine voice, "We're home." I believed that. As he said in his poem, "I Shall Not Leave These Prisoning Hills," he was one with this land, one with the forest, one with the mountain looming above our heads, one with every living creature that made its habitation here. The oneness was his deep connection with all else being carried forward in the river's flow.

The Bible sets forth a dominant image of "destination." It will be a place characterized by *more than enough*. The image is expressed primarily through food. There will be more than enough to eat, as in the abundance of the Garden of Eden, as in manna rained down from heaven to feed travelers in the wilderness. The Bible pictures a great banquet table where guests will find abundantly ample provisions. A crowd of five thousand will find five loaves and two fish enough, with baskets full left over. *Enough:* it is the most restless anxiety in the human spirit: money enough, security enough, love enough, status enough, strong enough, thin enough, attractive enough, time enough? It is our perpetual struggle. To come to terms with *enough* is to slay a multitude of inner dragons and to find peace. This is the Bible's portrait of our promised destination. I, therefore, read at Mr. Still's funeral Isaiah 55:1–5, the prophetic call to God's great banquet, and Mark 6: 30–44, Jesus's feeding of the multitude.

Mr. Still could be playful with religion. In discussing one of his poems, he said, "I had been wanting to write about those I want to be with me in heaven, wishing to have some fun describing my favorites. But then, as I finished, it occurred to me, why don't you add a little mischief? So I did! I entitled the poem 'Those I Want To Be with Me in Heaven, Should There Be Such a Place.'" His dark eyes gleamed with laughter as he related the incident.

His funeral called to mind the many hours Nancy and I had spent with him. There were our excursions to the log house to sit for an afternoon amid the primitive confines of his bachelor quarters discussing twentieth century literature and the people who had produced it. (Nancy has been a prolific reader all her life and felt right at home; I, far less so.) "Sure, I knew Sandburg, Robert Frost, Jessie Stuart, Marjorie Kinnan Rawlings, Harry Caudill." And then there was Joy Davidman, who would later become C.S. Lewis's wife, and, after her tragic early death to cancer, the central character in the drama "Shadowlands". Available to this day are copies of hand-typed letters sent by young Joy Davidman to Jim Still acclaiming the success of *River of Earth* in New York City and conveying the slightest hints of a flirtatious tease: "I would love to hide in your rhubarb patch."

There was the twenty-eight mile ride we took to Whitesburg one day for lunch at the Courthouse Restaurant. "The man who lived in that house right there murdered his wife and tried to flee into Ohio, but they caught him," Mr. Still said at one point. And a little further down the road, "That family right there raised sixteen children and graduated every last one of them from college." And "Several generations ago, the people on those two farms waged a blood feud over family honor and threatened to wipe out the whole population." State highway 160 was filled with human sagas still alive in Mr. Still's memory.

He would visit Louisville, always staying with Molly and Vernon Bundy. I would recruit him to read his poetry during worship at Highland Presbyterian Church. The poetry was wonderful but, above that, he was a mesmerizing presence. He would stand in the pulpit, gaze thoughtfully at the congregation and, in his typically understated mountain manner, read. It was a moment of awe, a time to sense down deep that you were in the presence of a master.

I carried Mr. Still one day to Atkinson Elementary School in Louisville's West End. Atkinson, with one hundred percent of its students qualifying for free breakfast and free lunch, was academically the lowest scoring of all fifty-two schools in the Louisville/Jefferson County elementary system. Before two assemblages of students, one first-through-third graders, and the other fourth and fifth graders, Mr. Still read from two of his children's works, "The Appalachian Mother Goose" and "Jack and the Wonder Beans." Mr. Still believed that two of the finest pieces of children's literature ever written in English were "Mother Goose" and "Jack and the Bean Stalk," and he wrote his own Eastern Kentucky version of each. The effect on five classes of urban ghetto children was the same as on educated, erudite Highland Presbyterian Church: awe! These squirmy, squirrely, low-attention-span kids sat glued, not understanding it all, but also not daring to miss anything. The questions afterward were typical of seven-year-olds, and Mr. Still seemed thoroughly at home in their world. With the classes over, we were ushered to the lunchroom for pizza and fruit, during which time one teacher came to thank Mr. Still for coming. "This was *wonderful*! We *never* have anyone like you here at our school." In the ride back to Molly Bundy's house, Mr. Still commented, "I'd like to be connected with a school like this, where the children don't have everything already." Quite a number of them could have been, not long before, his Knott County neighbors.

He told us the story of browsing through a used bookstore in the 1980s. He came upon a first edition, hardback copy of *River of Earth*, more than forty years old. "Not many of these left," he thought to himself; "I'll buy it." He looked inside the cover: five dollars. He carried it to the counter and handed it to the woman to make the purchase. "Oh, I'm sorry, Sir," she said, "This is a signed copy. It will cost you ten." Without a word, Mr. Still paid the ten dollars and left the store.

The funeral attendees were a gallery of Appalachian notables. There was Wilma Dykeman, a resident of Asheville, North Carolina, a central figure in Appalachian literary and political culture during the twentieth century. She authored eighteen books including *The French Broad*, *The Tall Woman*, *The Far Family*, and *Return the Innocent Earth*, and was always a leading proponent for the preservation of the French Broad River waterway. There was Ted Olson, who taught Appalachian studies and English at East Tennessee State University. There was Carol Boggess, professor of English at Mars Hill College in North Carolina, who would shortly set out to write a biography of James Still. There was Lee Smith, author of (at that time) eight novels including *Saving Grace, The Devil's Dream,* and *Fair and Tender Ladies*, who taught English at North Carolina State University and often taught a summer writing workshop at the Hindman Settlement School. There was Loyal Jones, faculty member and director for twenty-three years of the Appalachian Center at Berea College, and the author of several books on Appalachian culture. There was Silas House, young, upcoming novelist of such works as *Clay's Quilt*, *A Parchment of Leaves*, and *The Coal Tattoo*, depicting generations of life in more modern Appalachia. There was Jack Spadaro, for twenty years a mine safety inspector for the U.S. Department of the Interior until, under pressure from area politicians, he was terminated for doing his job too well. There was Herb E. Smith of Appalshop arts and education center in Whitesburg, Kentucky, the creator of more than ninety video documentaries about Appalachian people and their life. These and many others came. Amid all this accomplishment, who was I to be a leader in Mr. Still's funeral? I still wonder. But he always seemed to collect unlikely characters for his stories, so maybe I was just one more.

The friendship Nancy and I had with Mr. Still remains one of the immense treasures of our lives. Here was a highly prominent literary voice of twentieth century Appalachia, and we had the privilege of spending hours sounding out his mind and soul. He lived a simple, unpretentious life in the remote hills of Knott County, never owning much and never needing much. He traveled widely in his life, but "you got hillbilly wrote all over you" remained the best description of the man. To see him on a sidewalk in Whitesburg or in a hallway of the Hindman Settlement School was to evoke no special notice. But, for those who knew him, an aura surrounded him. His lifetime of reading, listening, writing, and associating with both ordinary people and literary giants set him apart. Hearing about his Knott County neighbors but also about his friendships with the great writers of his time was a rare gift. His minimalist style, powerful meaning conveyed through few words, marked both his writing and his conversation. His capacity to know intimately the human heart, its struggles, its unanswered questions, its great joys, and its profound frustrations, was his genius. His oneness with the ox, the fawn, the flowering shrub, the brook, and the mountain underlay the whole of his being. To know him was to join a much larger universe, moving endlessly at the river's pace. In our conversations, Nancy and I never wanted to miss a word or inflection because of the insight that might be revealed. Driving home after our visits, we consumed the five hours reviewing the day's talk, hoping not to forget anything.

To know a true literary genius was a pearl of exceptional value.